The Ethics of Whistleblowing

T0371800

Following the enormous political, legal, and media interest that has surrounded high profile cases of whistleblowing, such as Chelsea Manning and Edward Snowden, the fundamental ethical questions surrounding whistleblowing have often been obscured. In this fascinating book, Eric Boot examines the ethical issues at stake in whistleblowing.

Can the disclosure of classified government documents ever be justified? If so, how? Why does it require justification in the first place? Can there ever be a duty to blow the whistle? When is breaking the law justified?

On a more practical level, this book also considers the various whistleblower protection documents and finds them often lacking in consistency and clarity, before providing an argument for a plausible "public interest" defense for whistleblowers.

Eric R. Boot is a Lecturer at Utrecht University, The Netherlands. He is also the author of *Human Duties and the Limits of Human Rights Discourse* (2017).

Routledge Focus on Philosophy

Routledge Focus on Philosophy is an exciting and innovative new series, capturing and disseminating some of the best and most exciting new research in philosophy in short book form. Peer reviewed and, at a maximum of fifty thousand words, shorter than the typical research monograph, *Routledge Focus on Philosophy* titles are available in both ebook and print-on-demand format. Tackling big topics in a digestible format the series opens up important philosophical research for a wider audience, and as such is invaluable reading for the scholar, researcher and student seeking to keep their finger on the pulse of the discipline. The series also reflects the growing inter-disciplinarity within philosophy and will be of interest to those in related disciplines across the humanities and social sciences.

For more information about this series, please visit: www.routledge.com/ Routledge-Focus-on-Philosophy/book-series/RFP

The Ethics of Whistleblowing

Eric R. Boot

Routledge
Taylor & Francis Group

LONDON AND NEW YORK

First published 2019
by Routledge
4 Park Square, Milton Park, Abingdon, Oxon OX14 4RN
605 Third Avenue, New York, NY 10017

First issued in paperback 2023

Routledge is an imprint of the Taylor & Francis Group, an informa business

British Library Cataloguing-in-Publication Data
A catalogue record for this book is available from the British Library

Library of Congress Cataloging-in-Publication Data
Names: Boot, Eric R., 1984- author.
Title: The ethics of whistleblowing/Eric R. Boot.
Description: Abingdon, Oxon; New York: Routledge, 2019. |
Series: Routledge focus on philosophy | Includes bibliographical
references and index.
Identifiers: LCCN 2019007549 | ISBN 9781138343696 (hardback: alk. paper) |
ISBN 9780429439001 (e-book)
Subjects: LCSH: Public policy (Law)–Philosophy. | Whistle blowing–Law
and legislation–Philosophy. | Whistle blowing–Moral and ethical aspects.
Classification: LCC K378 .B66 2019 | DDC 172/.1–dc23
LC record available at https://lccn.loc.gov/2019007549

ISBN: 978-1-03-257057-0 (pbk)
ISBN: 978-1-138-34369-6 (hbk)
ISBN: 978-0-429-43900-1 (ebk)

DOI: 10.4324/9780429439001

Typeset in Times New Roman
by Deanta Global Publishing Services, Chennai, India

Publisher's Note
The publisher has gone to great lengths to ensure the quality of this reprint but
points out that some imperfections in the original copies may be apparent.

Contents

Acknowledgments

The research for this book was done in the context of the research project "Unauthorized Disclosures," which was part of the ERC-funded project "Democratic Secrecy: A Philosophical Analysis of the Role of Secrecy in Democratic Governance," led by Dorota Mokrosinska. So I would like to thank her, first of all, for the opportunity to spend several years thinking about the various ethical issues surrounding whistleblowing. I would like to thank as well my wonderful former colleagues at Leiden University for their helpful feedback and insights that, at one point or another, helped me order my thoughts and improve my writings. Furthermore, the various papers that this book is based on have been presented at numerous conferences in sundry forms. The helpful feedback I received there has been of tremendous importance in realizing the present work. In particular, I would like to thank Michele Bocchiola, Kimberley Brownlee, Jonathan Bruno, Simon Caney, Emanuela Ceva, Candice Delmas, Axel Gosseries, Manohar Kumar, Rahul Sagar, Will Smith, and Daniele Santoro. I hope my treatment of their remarks, concerns, and suggestions has done them justice and that the final result is the better for it.

In the final months before submitting the entire manuscript, I had the opportunity to enjoy a research stay at the UC Berkeley School of Law. This provided me both with the necessary time to finish the book and with the pleasure of discussing my work with Chris Kutz, whose helpful comments have certainly improved the work.

Finally, my profound gratitude goes out to my family – my wife Pina and my children Eleonora and Federico – simply for being there.

1 Introduction

Let us start with a case most readers will likely be familiar with: Edward Snowden's disclosures regarding the National Security Agency's (NSA) mass surveillance programs. Briefly discussing this case will allow me to introduce the general theme of this book, present some of its main questions, and clarify what the unique focus of the present work on whistleblowing is. Snowden downloaded and then passed on to journalists for *The Guardian* and *The Washington Post* (the former of which later enlisted the help of journalists for *ProPublica* and *The New York Times*) approximately 1.7 million U.S. government classified documents.[1] Among other things, these documents showed that Americans' phone and internet records were being monitored on a truly massive scale.[2] Hailed by some as a hero and reviled by others as a traitor, Snowden took it upon himself to disclose these documents to the public (via the above-mentioned journalistic outlets and after executing the necessary redactions). On the one hand, his revelations led to a U.S. District Court Judge finding the NSA's data collection program to be unconstitutional for violating the Fourth Amendment.[3] Similarly, a federal appellate court ruled that the NSA's bulk collection of communications records was illegal.[4] Furthermore, following Snowden's revelations, Congress passed the USA Freedom Act, which introduced vital reforms to the NSA's bulk data collection program. Shortly after Snowden's disclosures, moreover, the UN General Assembly declared online privacy to be a fundamental human right.[5] Finally, his disclosures sparked a great public debate worldwide concerning the fundamental values of privacy, security, and transparency. These facts seem to indicate that Snowden's disclosures did indeed reveal grave government wrongdoing and, therefore, truly served the "public interest" (a term to be further defined in Chapter 3).

On the other hand, some have pointed out that Snowden's disclosures have hampered the functioning of certain NSA programs that have actually played a role in preventing terrorist attacks. The President's Review Group on Intelligence and Communications Technologies concluded, for example, that Section 702 of the Foreign Intelligence Surveillance Act – allowing the U.S. intelligence community to target the communications of non-U.S. persons residing outside the United States for foreign intelligence purposes – has played a role in gathering the intelligence that led to over 50 counterterrorism investigations. The President's Review Group is convinced that Section 702 does in fact "play an important role in the nation's effort to prevent terrorist attacks across the globe."[6] Exposure of this program as a consequence of Snowden's disclosures may thus have inhibited its functioning.[7] Still, it remains an open question whether the success that (some of) the NSA's surveillance programs have had outweighs the costs to privacy.

Others have criticized Snowden for the unilateral manner in which he acted. As Seana Shiffrin put it, his disclosures did not merely amount to a political critique of the NSA's surveillance programs but were instead "political speech acts."[8] In other words, his disclosures did not merely constitute a *criticism* of particular policies, but rather they amounted to a unilateral political *decision*. Unauthorized disclosures such as Snowden's immediately, performatively as it were, undo the decision (made by democratically elected officials) to keep a certain piece of information secret. But who is this Booz Allen Hamilton contractor to decide for millions of Americans what ought to be public and what may remain secret? Is that not the task of our representatives in government?

This very brief discussion of the Snowden case shows us that it is by no means a straightforward matter to judge such cases and that, therefore, as I will argue in a moment, sustained philosophical reflection is required. Snowden's case is also a clear example of the type of whistleblowing that will be the focus of this book, which I will refer to as *classified public whistleblowing*: "classified" in the sense that *state* secrets are involved; "public" in the sense that the information is disclosed to the public (typically via the media), as opposed to an internal or external supervisory body. The reason for focusing on disclosures to the *public* is that they are, comparatively speaking, far more complex and difficult to judge (i.e., whether a particular unauthorized disclosure is justified) than the addressing of wrongdoing through the appropriate channels.[9] Indeed, often the stated goal of whistleblower protection legislation is to render the more problematic case of unauthorized disclosures unnecessary by providing for safe and legal options for addressing wrongdoing either internally or (if that fails or is expected to be fruitless) externally through the appropriate supervisory bodies.[10] When such legislation is in place and functioning properly, whistleblowing is a perfectly legal action that is morally fairly unproblematic.[11] Classified public whistleblowing, however, is an entirely different story. Because it typically involves breaking the law and the violation of a number of other obligations (promissory obligations, for example), it raises a whole different set of moral questions, which make it more akin to civil disobedience than to the legal forms of addressing wrongdoing (though it also differs from civil disobedience in significant ways, as we shall see in Chapter 4). Furthermore, the reason I focus on the disclosure of *state* (rather than corporate) secrets is that such disclosures in particular stand to benefit from the political philosophical treatment this book offers. Of course, I am aware that the public and the corporate do not always neatly come apart. Snowden himself, for example, was not a civil servant, but rather an employee of Booz Allen Hamilton. He worked as a subcontractor for the National Security Agency but was still employed by a private company. Nonetheless, however, Snowden's is a case of classified public whistleblowing as the secrets he disclosed were *state* secrets.

One final clarification of the scope of this book concerns the types of societies to which our examination of unauthorized disclosures is limited. This inquiry into whistleblowing only applies to what John Rawls referred to as "nearly just" states. What he meant was states with a democratic government and a constitutional regime that more or less satisfies the two principles of justice,[12] but in which nonetheless grave instances of injustice do occur. It is a state, furthermore, characterized by widespread support for its institutions (though of course citizens may not be in favor of the current government) and a publicly recognized conception of justice.[13] It is a state, in short, much like most Western liberal democratic states today. The reason for this focus is that several of the arguments offered in this book would need to be altered significantly in nonideal circumstances. For example, the argument for an obligation to blow the whistle, developed in Chapter 6, would need to be altered for a nonideal state. In such a state, the act of whistleblowing may actually put oneself and one's loved ones in physical danger, rendering such an obligation far too demanding. For this reason, the arguments applied in this work apply only to nearly just (or nearly ideal) states.

One can approach such whistleblowing[14] from sundry perspectives: many have approached disclosures such as Snowden's from a legal perspective,[15] inquiring into the (il)legality or the (un)constitutionality of particular disclosures, comparing existing whistleblower protection legislation in different countries, considering the flaws in existing secrecy laws and classification procedures, and at times proposing reforms to existing laws and policies. Advocacy groups, such as Transparency International, Open Society Foundations, and PEN American Center, survey the legal landscape as well but often add a sociological component (e.g., How do whistleblowers fare in different countries? How are they viewed in various countries?)

and of course an advocacy component, typically calling for greater transparency in government, a human right to know, and stronger and more reliable whistleblower protection laws.

Instead, the present work, though it is certainly informed by the work done by both legal scholars and advocacy groups, has a different approach to the question of whistleblowing; the questions it raises are chiefly *moral* in nature, such as: "What conditions need to be met for whistleblowing to be morally justified?"; "Why does whistleblowing require moral justification to begin with? Is it somehow morally wrongful?"; "Can there be a (legal and/or moral) right to whistleblowing?"; "Can one ever have a moral obligation to blow the whistle?"; "How do we deal with conflicting obligations (e.g., to prevent or end grave government wrongdoing by speaking out versus our promissory, role, and legal obligations to refrain from whistleblowing)?" Though this book will chiefly engage with these and similar questions, it will also relate the insights resulting from this moral inquiry to the legal reality concerning whistleblowers, at times even providing concrete suggestions for improvement.

A brief survey of existing laws, policies, and guidance documents concerning whistleblowing will quickly clarify why sustained philosophical analysis is urgently needed. As said, this work will be concerned not with internal whistleblowing or with addressing wrongdoing externally through the appropriate supervisory bodies, but rather with unauthorized disclosures of state secrets to the media. These difficult cases are often unsatisfactorily discussed in legal texts and policy documents. The Council of Europe's 2014 recommendation *Protection of Whistleblowers*, for example, simply states that a "special scheme or rules, including modified rights and obligations, may apply to information relating to national security, defence, intelligence, public order or international relations of the State."[16] The 2009 Dutch law concerning the addressing of wrongdoing by civil servants (including those in the intelligence community) did not even mention the option of public disclosure via the media.[17] The 2016 general Dutch whistleblower protection law states that whether disclosures to the media are to be protected will need to be decided on a case-by-case basis with the help of the case law of the European Court of Human Rights (ECtHR) and the above-cited recommendation of the Council of Europe.[18] The latter is of little help as it merely states that disclosures to the media ought to be protected "when necessary."[19] When such protection is necessary, however, is not clarified. As for the ECtHR's case law, it is (1) not always clear and (2) not always consistent on this point. Regarding the lack of clarity, in *Guja v. Moldova*, for example, the Court argues that unauthorized disclosures of secret government information should be protected, if they demonstrate "wrongdoing of public interest."[20] What exactly is to be understood by "wrongdoing of public interest" and why it justifies whistleblowing is not made clear however. Which disclosures serve the public interest, and which do not, thus remains an open question, the resolution of which largely depends on the judge(s) in question. The second problem – the Court's lack of consistency – becomes evident from the following: the same case of *Guja v. Moldova* argues that a report is only made in good faith if it is not motivated by resentment or the wish for personal gain.[21] However, three years later, the Court states, in *Heinisch v. Germany*, that Ms. Heinisch acted in good faith when reporting misconduct, even though she was partly driven by the desire to improve her own working conditions.[22] The ECtHR's case law will thus also not be a very reliable guide in deciding whether whistleblowers deserve protection.

Several judicial bodies and organizations have developed lists of criteria that are to be met for an unauthorized disclosure to be justified and thus to warrant protection. The problem is that these lists are not mutually consistent. For example, the lists provided by the Dutch whistleblower protection law[23] and the ECtHR do include a criterion of good faith, whereas others, such as the UK's *Public Interest Disclosure Act* (*PIDA*) and the Open Society Foundations' *Tshwane Principles*, do not.[24] In weighing the benefit (to the public interest) of a particular disclosure against the possible harm the disclosure could do, some of the lists only consider the possible harm to the public authority in question,[25] whereas others focus on the harm to the public interest,[26] whereas others still focus on harm to agents in the field.

The various lists, like the one provided by the ECtHR, furthermore, lack clarity as well, for example concerning the important matter of the understanding of the public interest that is employed. The clarification of this central concept is crucial. So long as it is not defined, applications of the public interest in whistleblowing cases remain *ad hoc*, threatening legal certainty. Not knowing what to expect – whether their disclosure will be considered in the public interest or not – potential whistleblowers might choose to err on the safe side and remain silent, thus depriving the public of important information concerning their government.

Despite all the mutual inconsistencies, the various lists do agree on one thing, namely that unauthorized disclosures to the media should only enjoy protection from retaliation if certain justifying conditions are met (though what the conditions are, is a matter of dispute, as we have seen). In other words, all agree that whistleblowing is a *pro tanto* wrongful act. None explain, however, why this should be so. It is the aim of Chapter 2, therefore, to explain what accounts for the *pro tanto* wrongfulness of whistleblowing. It will be argued that it is wrongful because it constitutes a violation of (1) promissory obligations, (2) role obligations,[27] and (3) the obligation to respect the democratic allocation of power. There is thus a *pro tanto* obligation to refrain from whistleblowing. Contrary to categorical obligations, *pro tanto* obligations are defeasible, however, and so are liable to be outweighed by countervailing moral reasons.

What might these reasons be? What, in other words, are the conditions that are to be met for whistleblowing to be justified all things considered? As we have already seen, the various legal and policy documents are mutually inconsistent and rather unclear on this matter. Accordingly, Chapter 3 develops three conditions that must be met for classified public whistleblowing to be morally justified. The first condition functions as a *threshold condition*, meaning that if it is not met the whole process of establishing the degree of justifiability of a given disclosure ends immediately. The threshold condition states that the disclosed information must serve the public interest, a term notoriously vague. In order to clarify the concept, I discuss and reject three common accounts of the public interest: the aggregative, procedural, and unitary accounts. As an alternative, I propose a *civic account* of the public interest, according to which public interests are those interests we share in our role as citizens.

The two remaining conditions concern the *manner* of disclosure. The *first procedural condition* is that of *ultimum remedium*: public disclosure must be a measure of last resort. Only if the whistleblower has first exhausted all alternative channels for addressing wrongdoing (or if pursuing these is judged to be fruitless, because they have been corrupted), may she proceed to disclose the classified information to the public. The *second procedural condition* requires the whistleblower to do all she can to *minimize the harmful consequences* of her disclosure. Notably absent from the justifying conditions provided in this chapter is that of good faith. The fact that Mark Felt (a.k.a. Deep Throat) did not have entirely or solely public-spirited motives does not mean that his disclosure of information regarding the Watergate scandal was any less in the public interest. The distinction made between the threshold condition and the procedural conditions, as well as the greater weight accorded to the former, allows me to view the wrongfulness (or justness) of a particular unauthorized disclosure as a matter of *degree*. Depending on which and how many (if any) of the justifying conditions are met, particular cases of whistleblowing will be judged more or less justified (or not justified at all). Such gradations of moral wrongfulness will serve us well when considering the legal consequences of (more or less) wrongful cases of whistleblowing.

If whistleblowing can indeed be morally justified (according to the conditions provided in Chapter 3), it ought to enjoy some measure of legal protection, lest a chilling effect cause potential whistleblowers to refrain from disclosing government wrongdoing in the future, leaving the public ignorant of the government's transgressions. Chapters 4 and 5 will, therefore, inquire what form a defense of justified whistleblowing should take. Chapter 4 discusses the most commonly proposed defense of whistleblowing, namely the defense based on the individual right to freedom of expression (understood broadly, as the right to seek, receive, use, and impart information). The main claim of this chapter will be a negative one, namely that a defense of whistleblowing cannot be based on individual *rights*, be they legal or moral.

A more promising defense is discussed in Chapter 5. Recall the threshold condition (expounded in Chapter 3) that all justified whistleblowing must meet: the unauthorized disclosure must be *in the public interest*. Accordingly, this chapter proposes a *public interest defense*. This would be a criminal defense for whistleblowers, meaning that the prohibition of disclosing government secrets remains in place, but that under certain conditions the violation of that prohibition is deemed justified. Depending on whether all or only one or two of the justifying conditions (developed in Chapter 3) are met, this *justification defense* can function either as a full defense or as a sentencing mitigation factor. Such a defense of (partially) justified whistleblowing would achieve a felicitous balance between, on the one hand, recognizing the importance of democratic authority and preventing undesirable acts (i.e., frivolous and willfully false disclosures) and, on the other hand, providing protection for justified cases of whistleblowing, so that the latter may continue to perform its vital public function of bringing grave government wrongdoing to light and thus calling authority to account when it oversteps its limits.

Finally, Chapter 6 asks whether there can ever be an obligation to blow the whistle. This question is typically neglected, as scholars tend to focus on the question of whistleblowing's permissibility. Furthermore, I suspect, many feel a certain unease about the notion of an *obligation* to blow the whistle. Often, supporters of whistleblowers paint them in heroic colors, as selfless servants of the common good who sacrifice a great deal in the name of justice. And, indeed, many whistleblowers have suffered grave consequences for their actions, including dismissal, personal harassment, blacklisting, transfer, and criminal charges. For this reason, I believe (and I have found many a time when presenting on this topic at conferences), many resist any talk of an *obligation* to engage in whistleblowing. They consider the act of whistleblowing to be above and beyond the call of duty, that is, an act of supererogation. Nonetheless, Chapter 6 presents the argument that there is at least one case in which we may speak of obligatory whistleblowing without running afoul of concerns about being overdemanding, namely the obligation to blow the whistle on wrongdoing in which one is (or has been) oneself complicit. Specifically, I argue that civil servants who are complicit in government wrongdoing incur a *moral obligation* to remedy the wrongdoing to which they have contributed by blowing the whistle on it. This obligation, however, is defeasible, and its strength (and thus the likelihood of its being defeated) depends on the blameworthiness of one's complicity.

In brief, this book sets out to provide some conceptual and normative clarity concerning the key normative issues surrounding the phenomenon of classified public whistleblowing. By examining these issues, this book furthermore wishes to make up for the great dearth of philosophical reflection on the dynamic social, legal, and political phenomenon that is classified public whistleblowing, which regrettably lags significantly behind the great outpouring of both popular and academic writings on the subject in other fields.

Notes

1 Strohm, Chris, and Del Quentin Wilber. 2014. Pentagon Says Snowden Took Most US Secrets Ever: Rogers. *Bloomberg News*, January 10. Retrieved from: https://www.bloomberg.com/news/articles/2014-01-09/pentagon-finds-snowden-took-1-7-million-files-rogers-says.
2 Consider that "for a thirty-day period ending in February 2013, one unit of the NSA collected more than *three billion* pieces of communication data from US communication systems alone" (Greenwald, Glenn. 2015. *No Place to Hide: Edward Snowden, the NSA and the Surveillance State*. London: Penguin Books. 30).
3 Gerstein, Josh. 2013. Judge: NSA Program Likely Unconstitutional. *Politico*, December 12.
4 Stempel, Jonathan. 2015. NSA's Phone Spying Program Ruled Illegal by Appeals Court. *Reuters*, May 7.
5 United Nations General Assembly. *The Right to Privacy in the Digital Age*. UN. Doc A/RES/68/167 (December 18, 2013).
6 The President's Review Group on Intelligence and Communications Technologies. 2013. *Liberty and Security in a Changing World*. December 12. 144–5.
7 Benkler, Yochai. 2014. A Public Accountability Defense for National Security Leakers and Whistleblowers. *Harvard Law and Policy Review* 8: 281–326. 322. Benkler, however, maintains that data collection under Section 702 greatly affects the lives of both innocent civilians abroad and American citizens and thus requires democratic debate.
8 Shiffrin, Seana. 2017. The Moral Neglect of Negligence. In *Oxford Studies in Political Philosophy. Volume 3*. Eds. David Sobel, Peter Vallentyne, and Steve Wall, 197–228. Oxford: Oxford University Press. 208.
9 On addressing wrongdoing through the appropriate internal and external channels see Ceva, Emanuela, and Michele Bocchiola. 2018. Personal Trust, Public

Accountability, and the Justification of Whistleblowing. *Journal of Political Philosophy*. Advance online publication. doi: 10.1111/jopp.12170.

10 Thus the 2016 Dutch whistleblower protection law was intended, among other things, to render disclosures to the media superfluous by providing for safe alternatives to voice one's concerns about possible wrongdoing: Voorstel van wet van de leden Van Raak, Fokke, Schouw, Segers, Ouwehand en Klein tot wijziging van de Wet Huis voor klokkenluiders (Proposal for an amendment of the Dutch Whistleblowing Protection Law), *Kamerstukken (Parliamentary Papers) II* 2014/15, 34105, 7, p. 23.

11 Though of course the existence of such whistleblower protection legislation cannot always prevent the occurrence of *informal* sanctions (e.g., being transferred to a different department, being shut out from important meetings, or being shunned by one's colleagues).

12 Rawls, John. 1999. *A Theory of Justice*. Revised ed. Cambridge (Mass.): Belknap Press of Harvard University Press. 310.

13 Ibid. 339.

14 From now on, when I write "whistleblowing" I will intend "classified public whistleblowing," unless indicated otherwise.

15 In the American context, see, e.g., Benkler 2014; Fenster, Mark. 2012. Disclosure's Effects: WikiLeaks and Transparency. *Iowa Law Review* 97: 753–807; Kitrosser, Heidi. 2008. Classified Information Leaks and Free Speech. *University of Illinois Law Review* 2008: 881–931; Pozen, David E. 2010. Deep Secrecy. *Stanford Law Review* 62: 257–339. In the European context, see: Kagiaros, Dimitrios. 2015. Protecting "National Security" Whistleblowers in the Council of Europe: An Evaluation of Three Approaches on How to Balance National Security with Freedom of Expression. *The International Journal of Human Rights* 19: 408–28; Voorhoof, Dirk. 2015. Freedom of Journalistic News-Gathering, Access to Information and Protection of Whistle-Blowers under Article 10 ECHR and the Standards of the Council of Europe. In *Journalism at Risk: Threats, Challenges and Perspectives*, 105–40. Strasbourg: Council of Europe Publishing.

16 Committee of Ministers of the Council of Europe. Protection of Whistleblowers: Recommendation CM/Rec(2014)7 and explanatory memorandum. 7. Available at: https://rm.coe.int/16807096c7

17 Binnenlandse Zaken. Besluit melden vermoeden van misstand bij Rijk en Politie (Decree regulating the addressing of wrongdoing by civil servants) (2009).

18 *Kamerstukken II* 2014/15, 23.

19 Council of Europe 2014, 14.

20 European Court of Human Rights (ECtHR) (Grand Chamber). *Guja v. Moldova*. February 12, 2008. Application no. 14277/04. § 74. The Court uses a total of six criteria to judge particular restrictions of whistleblowers' right to freedom of expression under Article 10 of the European Convention of Human Rights.

21 ECtHR. *Guja v. Moldova*. § 77.

22 ECtHR. *Heinisch v. Germany*. July 21, 2011. Application no. 28274/08. § 83.

23 Staatsblad van het Koninkrijk der Nederlanden. Jaargang 2016. *Wet Huis voor klokkenluiders*. Article 18.

24 "The motivation for a protected disclosure is irrelevant except where the disclosure is proven to be knowingly untrue." (Open Society Foundations. 2013. *The Global Principles on National Security and the Right to Information (Tshwane Principles)*. Available at: https://www.opensocietyfoundations.org/publications/

global-principles-national-security-and-freedom-information-tshwane-principles. Principle 38b.)
25 ECtHR. *Guja v. Moldova*. § 76.
26 *Tshwane Principles*. Principle 43b.
27 Though role obligations, as I understand them, do not proscribe whistleblowing if the information disclosed serves the public interest, as we will see.

2   A *pro tanto* wrong[1]

One of the tasks to be undertaken in Chapter 3 – the clarification of the conditions that need to be met for whistleblowing to be morally and legally justified – presupposes that whistleblowing is something that requires justification; that is, that whistleblowing is wrongful unless certain conditions are met. It is the aim of the present chapter to explain what it is that renders whistleblowing (*pro tanto*) wrongful.

Scholars provide sundry reasons for viewing classified public whistleblowing as wrongful. One could argue that it (1) hurts *national security*,[2] (2) inhibits the *adequate and efficient functioning of government*, which requires loyalty on the part of civil servants,[3] or (3) could damage reputations and violate the privacy of or be otherwise *harmful* to third persons.[4] Alternatively, one might argue that (4) the unauthorized disclosure of classified material constitutes a *breach of promissory obligations*, as civil servants are generally required to sign a confidentiality agreement.[5] Closely connected to this point, some might say that (5) whistleblowing appears to be in *conflict with one's role responsibilities*, such as the civil servant's role obligation of obedience.[6] Finally, one could maintain that (6) such whistleblowing is *at odds with democratic authority*, that is, classified public whistleblowers exercise discretionary power concerning what is and is not to be a state secret, which properly belongs to the executive elected by the people.[7]

In my view, the first three points do not establish the *pro tanto* wrongful nature of classified public whistleblowing or a *pro tanto* obligation[8] to refrain from whistleblowing. Rather, they can lead us to place certain restraints on the *manner in which* one goes about disclosing classified information. They present us with a duty to exercise great care when disclosing classified information (of which I will say more in the next chapter), rather than simply forbidding us to engage in whistleblowing in general.

Nothing similar can be said of the latter three points. My promissory obligation does not merely constrain the *way in which* I break my promise;

rather, it commands me not to break my promise. Similarly, my role obligation and the obligation to respect the democratic allocation of power for-
bid me to disclose classified government documents *tout court*, rather than
merely limit the *manner in which* I disclose them. It is thus the latter three
points that seem to account for the *pro tanto* wrongful nature of classified
public whistleblowing. Let us discuss each in turn.

2.1 Promissory obligations

Civil servants are often made to swear an oath to respect the confidential
nature of certain documents they encounter in the course of their work.
Consequently, classified public whistleblowing can be considered *pro tanto*
wrongful, because it constitutes a breach of promissory obligations. For reasons of space I cannot, unfortunately, delve into the vast debate concerning
promises and how they give rise to obligations,[9] so instead I will merely
provide one example of an argument (largely Kantian in nature) one could
give in order to explain why we have an obligation to keep our promises.
For Kant, breaking one's promise is a violation of a perfect duty, as the
maxim (that is, the subjective principle of action) governing this action cannot even reasonably be *conceived* as a universal law.[10] After all, if the maxim
"I will make false promises whenever it suits my purposes" were to become
a universal law, the very condition of promising, namely that the promisee
believes the promisor will keep their promise, would disappear.[11] Rawls's
account of promissory obligations is conceived largely along these same
lines, but framed in terms of the duty of fair play, that is: as you benefit
from a just institution of promising, when you make a promise under this
institution you incur an obligation to uphold the institution by keeping your
promise, lest you become a free rider.[12]

In what follows, I will understand promissory obligations to be *content-
independent*, meaning that the source of the obligation does not lie in the
desirability of the act one promises to perform (i.e., in the promise's *content*) but instead simply in the fact that a promise was made. In other words,
the acts one is obligated to perform as a consequence of one's promise, "are
not justified by giving reasons for the desirability of each obligatory act in
its particular circumstances," but rather "by the justification of the general
norm that promises [...] ought to be respected."[13]

Recently, however, several philosophers in the civil disobedience debate
have challenged the idea that promises give rise to an obligation to keep
them. Both Candice Delmas and Kimberley Brownlee, for example, set
out to deny that government employees are bound by promises not to disclose classified information by rejecting the argument that freely made
promises bind us morally, "irrespective of the content of these promises."[14]

Now, of course, we can partially concede the point: to say that promise-making has normative consequences is not to say one could promise to do anything, however deplorable, and be considered under obligation to make good on one's promise, even if that would involve grave wrongdoing. It is an old and well-established point that promising to do something or granting one's consent to someone does not always put one under obligation.[15] This is not, however, an argument demonstrating that the content-independence view of promissory obligations is mistaken; rather, it shows that this view functions within certain normative constraints. Thus, as Raz, we might say that in order for a promise to do X to be binding, X must not be "grossly immoral."[16] Yet, given that the number of such limitations restricting the scope of the content-independence view is quite small and easily recognizable, we may nonetheless refer to promissory obligations as content-independent, with this caveat understood.[17]

Furthermore, stating that promise-making results in the promisor taking on obligations is not to say that these obligations are absolute. We could argue that promissory obligations are defeasible, *pro tanto* obligations and, as such, are liable to be defeated by countervailing moral reasons. Returning to our topic, it is one thing to say that the potential whistleblower's promise of confidentiality may be overridden by more pressing moral reasons (such as the public interest in disclosing grave government wrongdoing), but it is an entirely different matter to say that the whistleblower is not in the least presented with a moral conflict (because her promise of confidentiality was not morally binding to begin with).

Brownlee puts forward another argument against promissory obligations. She argues that there can be no "*pro tanto* content-insensitive moral obligation to conform to formal expectations [of an office] because we have sworn, consented, or otherwise committed ourselves to carrying out its functions,"[18] because "no decision to take up an office could be so well-informed, so prescient, that it could bind us to follow the dictates of the office no matter what issues arise."[19] Once again, I agree that not *all* promises put one under a *pro tanto* obligation to keep them. Promises to kill an innocent person, for example, or to perform other clearly morally reprehensible acts, are not binding (as argued above). It must be pointed out, however, that there is a significant difference between promising to do a, by definition, immoral act (like killing an innocent person) and promising to respect the confidential nature of certain government documents. The latter promise does not, in principle, bind one to perform morally reprehensible acts, particularly since my examination of unauthorized disclosures is limited to "nearly just" states (as noted in the previous chapter).

Nevertheless, there may be situations (even in a nearly just state), which one cannot foresee, in which one is commanded to keep manifestly unjust acts secret, or circumstances may occur in which the scope of secrecy has reached such bounds as to threaten the democratic nature of our polity as such. In such cases, one may appeal to weightier moral reasons that preponderate over one's promissory obligation, justifying its violation. But, in principle, the obligation to keep one's promise to respect state secrecy is a perfectly fine *pro tanto* content-independent obligation. Otherwise, if we follow Brownlee's reasoning, there can never be *pro tanto* content-independent obligations resulting from promises, even when they concern the performance of the most harmless acts, because we can never entirely foresee to what (possibly harmful) actions our promise will bind us in the future. So, for example, my promise to pick up my daughter from school does not lead to a *pro tanto* content-insensitive obligation to pick her up, because perhaps honoring my promise will involve turning away a student who is in urgent need of help with her thesis, or disregarding the request of a friend, who I know is going through a painful divorce and really needs some support, to pass by his house. This seems profoundly implausible. Of course, my promise *could* be overridden by a weightier or more pressing moral duty – e.g. to save a drowning child from a pond I pass by on my way to my daughter's school – but this does not mean my promise to my daughter does not generate a *pro tanto* moral obligation.

Finally, viewing the breach of promissory obligations as one of the reasons for judging classified public whistleblowing to be *pro tanto* wrongful allows us to understand the difference in treatment between whistleblowers and journalists. Classified public whistleblowers are often treated harshly, whereas, according to the American legal scholar Geoffrey Stone, the United States government has never in its history prosecuted a member of the press for publishing classified government information.[20] Indeed, American legal scholars seem to agree that the right to freedom of expression protects unauthorized disclosures of classified information by the press from criminal punishment unless the disclosure would result in "likely, imminent, and serious harm to the national security"[21] that is, furthermore, "specific" and "identifiable."[22] One obvious difference between the two that could account for this difference in treatment is that whistleblowers have breached a promissory obligation to respect the classified nature of state secrets, whereas the members of the press were under no such obligation. Moreover, journalists can be considered to be discharging their role obligation to inform the public about matters of fundamental public concern.[23]

2.2 Role obligations

Another possible reason for considering unauthorized disclosures of classified documents to be *pro tanto* wrongful is that they violate certain role obligations one has as a civil servant. "Role obligations" are hereby understood as a particular species of the genus "special obligations." Role obligations do not pertain to all persons; instead, their scope is limited to those who have taken on a particular role, e.g. the role of civil servant.[24] Furthermore, the content of role obligations is determined by the institutional role in question. Finally, the normative force of role obligations issues from the role itself.[25] Role obligations do not, in other words, rely on external justification, that is, on being prescribed by external moral rules.[26] It is for this reason that a role agent, say a civil servant, may be obligated to perform an act she considers to be wrongful. In such a case, the norms of her institutional role command her to perform a particular action, which she, on the basis of external moral norms, rejects. In order to see why this may be so, we need to clarify the role responsibility of civil servants.

The traditional understanding of civil servants' role responsibility is adequately summed up by Max Weber:

> The honor of the civil servant is vested in his ability to execute conscientiously the order of the superior authorities, exactly as if the order agreed with his own conviction. This holds even if the order appears wrong to him and if, despite the civil servant's remonstrances, the authority insists on the order. Without this moral discipline and self-denial, in the highest sense, the whole apparatus would fall to pieces.[27]

This *classical view of role responsibility*[28] essentially states that civil servants owe their superiors strict obedience. Their own political preferences and moral convictions are to play no part in the execution of their tasks. They ought to be impartial and to serve each administration equally well. This view of civil servants' role obligations has two important advantages: first, political accountability (democratic control) is enhanced. Policymakers can only be fully accountable if they can trust that their policy plans are being put into effect by civil servants just as they (the policymakers) had intended them. Second, the reliable and predictable execution of policy serves as a guarantee for legal certainty.[29] Policy is implemented by a great number of civil servants. If each of them would act according to her own convictions instead of in accordance with certain institutional guidelines, chaos would likely ensue, leaving citizens unsure regarding what they can expect of their government and of their fellow citizens, as well as what others (including the government) may rightfully expect of them, thus endangering legal certainty. Strict compliance with guidelines given by superiors, by contrast, functions as a guarantee against arbitrariness and can thus help establish a basis for legal certainty.

The classical view, however, does have one major drawback. It presupposes more or less just policies and integrious higher officials. If, by contrast, the policies are unjust or the higher officials corrupt, the civil servant's role obligation of obedience becomes highly problematic and can have grievous consequences. In such nonideal circumstances, one might argue, civil servants' role obligations ought instead to be characterized by loyalty to their own conscience; in other words, their role prescribes that in such circumstances they do what they themselves consider to be most just, rather than simply obey their superiors and trust their judgment.

In reply, I would first point out that I am interested in the issue of whistleblowing in nearly ideal circumstances, in which the state is reasonably just and democratic, policy is generally drafted with a view to the public interest, and officials are mostly not corrupt, but in which, nevertheless, cases of grave injustice may still occur. In such circumstances, as has been made clear, having civil servants obey their own conscience whenever they disagree with a given policy could threaten democratic accountability and legal certainty. Therefore, this second conception of civil servants' role obligations (the *personal conviction view*[30]), as consisting primarily in loyalty to one's own conscience and moral convictions, will not serve for the kind of nearly just state we are interested in.

The second point I would like to make in reply is more substantial, namely that civil servants' role obligations are not morally binding if the state that employs them is unjust. Consequently, we do not need the personal conviction view to justify disobeying the commands of an unjust regime, because the role obligations in such a case do not morally bind the role-occupants anyway. After all, not all roles, and not all institutions that engender roles, can be morally justified. It follows that the role obligations that flow from those roles are not morally justified either and, therefore, do not bind the role-occupants. For example, occupying the role "mobster" does not give rise to a moral obligation to break people's legs if they do not pay back their loan on time. The reason for this is that role morality cannot justify the imposition of role obligations if the role itself, or the institution engendering the role, cannot be justified.[31] In short, if the role of civil servant cannot be morally justified because the institution that gives rise to the role (i.e., the state) is profoundly unjust, then the obligations that flow from that role do not bind the role-occupant (i.e., the civil servant).[32]

Still, although we have excluded the possibility of civil servants having role obligations in an unjust regime, this does not entirely do away with the problem that the personal conviction view of role responsibility is thought to solve. After all, even in nearly just states civil servants may be confronted with policies that are gravely unjust. When they are commanded to help draft and implement such policies, ought they not to listen to their conscience and disobey? I argue that, yes, in cases of grave injustice civil servants may be justified in disobeying, but that they ought not to justify such disobedience by appealing to personal moral convictions. Rather, they ought to put forward *public* reasons for their disobedience.

This brings us to the third way we may conceive of civil servants' role obligations – the *civic conception of role responsibility*,[33] which avoids the trappings of granting primacy to one's private convictions but can also evade the problematic aspects of the classical view of role obligations. According to this conception, the civil servant owes loyalty, in the last instance, neither to her superiors or the serving government nor to her own conscience, but rather to the democratic constitutional state as such. In practice, this means that any time she disobeys a command from her superiors she ought to justify that disobedience by appealing to the *public interest* (to be further defined in the following chapter). The advantage of this view compared to the "strict obedience" conception should be clear: it leaves room for disobedience in those cases in which obeying orders would amount to harm to the public interest. Furthermore, the civic conception also has a clear advantage over the personal conviction view. As the only acceptable ground for disobedience is some threat to the public interest, the reasons one gives for one's disobedience ought also to be *public* reasons. These reasons, in other words, have to be general in form so that they *may be* acceptable to all (which is not to say that they *will be*; after all, people may reasonably disagree about what is in the public interest). They are truly *political* reasons and as such differ from reasons based on one's own personal *moral* or *religious* convictions that may justify disobedience according to the personal conviction view. Disobedience based on such "comprehensive doctrines" (as Rawls would call them) is incapable of public justification, given the pluralistic nature of our contemporary polities.

According to the civic conception of civil servants' role obligations, which I endorse, one's ultimate responsibility as a civil servant is to the democratic constitutional state as such. As a rule, one best fulfills this responsibility as a public official by obeying one's superiors, given the important advantages to democratic accountability and legal certainty mentioned above. Civil servants are thus role obligated to comply with superiors' orders, including orders to respect the secret nature of certain documents. Consequently, they are role obligated to refrain from disclosing state secrets. When obeying orders would constitute a grave threat to the public interest, however, obedience does not best serve the democratic constitutional state.[34] In such a case, therefore, civil servants[35] are not role obligated to obey.[36] In other words, if a disclosure is in the public interest (that is, if it better serves the democratic constitutional state than the alternative (remaining silent)), then a civil servant's role obligation, on this account, does not render such a disclosure wrongful at all (*pro tanto* or otherwise). In such a case, there is no role obligation to refrain from whistleblowing that is outweighed by countervailing moral reasons; rather there is no role obligation to refrain from whistleblowing to begin with. Role obligations, therefore, do not militate against unauthorized disclosures if the information disclosed reveals grave government wrongdoing.

2.3 The obligation to respect the democratic allocation of power

A third reason one might consider whistleblowing a *pro tanto* wrong is that it violates the duty to respect the democratic allocation of power. By way of explaining this duty, I will discuss Kant's argument, in the *Doctrine of Right*, for the natural duty of right to enter the state. For our purposes, we need not retrace all the intricacies of this argument. Instead, it will suffice to consider his point that the main function of the state is to do away with the situation in which multiple private conceptions of justice vie for dominance. Given that in this situation, the state of nature, we are all equally authoritative judges, no individual may claim the authority to serve as judge on another person's behalf. It follows that no individual may unilaterally assert rights and demand from others that they accept the correlative duties to respect those rights. As the unilateral assertion of rights cannot put others under obligation,[37] our rights in this condition can only be provisional.[38] In a situation in which each of us asserts her own contested set of provisional rights, none of us can be secure in our rights. Such a situation is deprived of justice, as it is a state in which "rights are in *dispute*."[39] The problem resides in each of us taking our own understanding of justice as guiding for all others. In the absence of a publicly defined set of laws specifying our rights and duties, each of us remains subject only to one's own private conception of justice, which, however, others are not obligated to regard as binding. As "no particular will can be legislative for a commonwealth,"[40] the solution, Kant argues, must lie in all of us surrendering our right to act in accordance with our own conception of justice and recognizing that "only the concurring and united will of all [...] can be legislative."[41] Only such an omnilateral will can solve the problems that arise as a consequence of each of us attempting to impose duties on others according to our own private judgment. Only a state, in other words, can solve the problem of some of us being subjected to the will of others and thus unfree. It does this by supplanting the great many understandings of justice by *one* that is to be binding for all. Or, as Anna Stilz puts it: "if we want to possess claims that, as objective rights, are actually respected by others in the external world, we will need to recognize *one and only one* common set of rules about rights, not a variety of competing private interpretations that coercively struggle for the upper hand."[42] No longer will individuals decide for themselves, but the community, as a whole, decides for all.

So how does this discussion pertain to our discussion of whistleblowing? I have said that protecting the rights of all requires the surrender of our natural right to act in accordance with our own understanding of justice to the state, which is to be guided by the collective lawgiving will. Now, if this collective lawgiving will has reached a consensus on certain limits to our freedom, one does wrong – to the community as a whole – by transgressing those limits. It is this train of thought that compels us to view classified public whistleblowing as wrongful: whistleblowers usurp the power to decide what does and does not fall within the bounds of legitimate state secrecy, whereas this is properly the prerogative of our democratically elected officials. These officials have received a mandate from the people to decide upon matters of state secrecy, whereas those involved in unauthorized disclosures have been elected neither by the people nor by its representatives. As Rahul Sagar puts it: "when unauthorized disclosures occur, vital decisions on matters of national security are effectively being made by private actors, an outcome that violates the democratic ideal that such decisions should be made by persons or institutions that have been directly or indirectly endorsed by citizens."[43]

2.4 Conclusion

We have discussed three possible reasons for viewing classified public whistleblowing as a *pro tanto* wrong: it constitutes a breach of (1) promissory obligations, (2) role obligations, and (3) the obligation to respect the democratic allocation of power. We saw, furthermore, that civil servants' role obligations actually do not militate against disclosure if that disclosure reveals grave government wrongdoing, at least according to the civic conception of civil servants' role responsibility I have argued for here. The other possible reasons for the wrongfulness of whistleblowing – that it could hurt national security, inhibit the adequate and efficient functioning of government, or cause harm to others – are, in fact, merely criteria for *how* a justified whistleblower ought to disclose information, not *whether* such whistleblowing is morally justifiable. These criteria, in other words, express *prudential* concerns rather than *normative* worries, as will be made clear in the following chapter.

20 *A pro tanto wrong*

Notes

1 This chapter draws from Boot, Eric R. 2017. Classified Public Whistleblowing: How to Justify a *pro tanto* Wrong. *Social Theory and Practice* 43: 541–67.
2 Sagar, Rahul. 2013. *Secrets and Leaks: The Dilemma of State Secrecy*. Princeton: Princeton University Press. 108.
3 Ibid. 110.
4 Bovens, Mark. 1998. *The Quest for Responsibility: Accountability and Citizenship in Complex Organisations*. Cambridge: Cambridge University Press. 195; Delmas, Candice. 2015. The Ethics of Government Whistleblowing. *Social Theory and Practice* 41: 77–105. 89ff.
5 Delmas. *Ethics of Government Whistleblowing*. 84ff.
6 Bok, Sissela. 1988. Whistleblowing and Professional Responsibilities. In *Ethical Issues in Professional Life*, Ed. Joan C. Callahan, 331–40. New York: Oxford University Press. 331.
7 Sagar. *Secrets and Leaks*. 116–17; Sagar, Rahul. 2007. On Combating the Abuse of State Secrecy. *The Journal of Political Philosophy* 15: 404–27. 424; Delmas. *Ethics of Government Whistleblowing*. 94.
8 *Pro tanto* obligations are defeasible obligations, which may be defeated by weightier countervailing moral reasons. Such reasons may justify the breaching of our *pro tanto* obligations.
9 For an excellent overview of the state of the art concerning research on promise-making, see Sheinman, Hanoch, Ed. 2011. *Promises and Agreements: Philosophical Essays*. Oxford: Oxford University Press.
10 Kant, Immanuel. 1996. Groundwork of The Metaphysics of Morals. In *Practical Philosophy*. Ed. Mary Gregor, Trans. Mary Gregor, 37–108. Cambridge: Cambridge University Press. Ak 4: 424.
11 Ibid. Ak 4: 422.
12 Rawls, John. 1999. *A Theory of Justice*. Revised ed. Cambridge (Mass.): Belknap Press of Harvard University Press. 305.
13 Raz, Joseph. 1972. Voluntary Obligations and Normative Powers. *Proceedings of the Aristotelian Society* 46: 79–102. 98. I do not have the space here to make an elaborate case for the content-independence view of promissory obligations, but would still like to offer one argument for it. That the obligations promises give rise to do not result from the promise's content becomes clear when we consider promises to perform morally neutral acts (i.e., acts one normally does not have a duty to perform): through the act of promising, these *adiaphora* suddenly become obligatory acts, demonstrating that their bindingness does not depend on the content of the promise, but simply on the fact that a promise was made.
14 Delmas. *Ethics of Government Whistleblowing*. 85; Brownlee, Kimberley. 2012. *Conscience and Conviction: The Case for Civil Disobedience*. Oxford: Oxford University Press. 112.
15 To give but a few historical examples from widely diverging philosophical schools: John Locke argues that one cannot, by contract or by one's own consent, transfer to any person (or authority) rights over oneself one does not possess. Thus, I cannot promise another person that I will become her slave in one year's time, nor do I incur an obligation to submit myself to her (Locke, John. 1988. *Two Treatises of Government*. Edited by Peter Laslett. Cambridge: Cambridge University Press. Bk. II, sec. 23. 284). Similarly, Kant argues that one cannot contract one's freedom away, as one would thereby bargain away the very

condition of promising and contracting, namely one's personhood. Such a promise or contract is, therefore, self-contradictory and does not yield any obligations (*Kant. Metaphysics of Morals.* Ak 6: 283). Beccaria argues against the death penalty by arguing that one cannot possibly grant others (through consent) the right to kill her, even upon committing the gravest offense. It would seem to follow that one can also incur no obligation as a consequence of such a promise (Beccaria, Cesare. 2010. *Dei delitti e delle pene.* Milan: Feltrinelli. Chapter 28. 80.

16 Raz, Joseph. 2006. The Problem of Authority: Revisiting the Service Conception. *Minnesota Law Review* 90: 1003–44. 1013.

17 Cf. Klosko, George. 2011. Are Political Obligations Content Independent? *Political Theory* 39: 498–523. 503.

18 Brownlee. *Conscience and Conviction.* 111.

19 Ibid. 112.

20 Stone, Geoffrey R. 2007. Government Secrecy vs. Freedom of the Press. *Harvard Law and Policy Review* 1: 185–217. 185–6. Consider, for example, the difference in treatment between the whistleblower Edward Snowden and the journalist Glenn Greenwald who made the information public through his articles in *The Guardian.* Snowden has been charged with two counts under the Espionage Act and with theft of government property, whereas Greenwald has not been charged.

21 Stone. Government Secrecy. 204; cf. Benkler, Yochai. 2011. A Free Irresponsible Press: Wikileaks and the Battle Over the Soul of the Networked Fourth Estate. *Harvard Civil Rights-Civil Liberties Law Review* 46: 311–97. 353.

22 Kitrosser, Heidi. 2008. Classified Information Leaks and Free Speech. *University of Illinois Law Review* 2008: 881–931. 928.

23 See, e.g., Harris, Nigel G.E. 1990. Journalists: A Moral Law unto Themselves? *Journal of Applied Philosophy* 7: 75–85.

24 Wueste, Daniel E. 1991. Taking Role Moralities Seriously. *The Southern Journal of Philosophy* 29: 407–17. 408.

25 Hardimon, Michael O. 1994. Role Obligations. *The Journal of Philosophy* 91: 333–63. 334.

26 Some would dispute this claim. A. John Simmons, for example, views the prescriptions of a particular role to be morally neutral. He argues they can only be morally binding on us if there is an external justification of the obligation in question, which is independent of the role prescribing the obligation (Simmons, A. John. 1979. *Moral Principles and Political Obligations.* Princeton: Princeton University Press. 16–23). Such a reductionist approach to our role obligations, however, is inadequate, as becomes evident when we consider involuntarily assumed roles, such as being a son or brother. The reductionist would have to account for the normative force of our duties to our parents (or siblings) by taking recourse to more general obligation – generating principles, such as consent, promise-making, gratitude, or some supposedly fair distribution of costs and benefits within the family. By contrast, non-reductionists would maintain that the sole source of our duties to our parents and siblings is our role as son or brother. For most people it is sufficient to point out that one stands in a certain relationship to a particular family member to justify the obligations we have towards her. Requiring an additional reason for the normative force of such duties seems to involve what Bernard Williams famously called "one thought too many."

27 Weber, Max. 1991. Politics as a Vocation. In *Essays in Sociology*. Ed. H.H. Gerth and C. Wright Mills, Trans. H.H. Gerth and C. Wright Mills, 77–128. London: Routledge. 95.
28 My discussion of the various ways one can understand the role responsibility of civil servants loosely draws on Mark Bovens's work on the subject: Bovens. *Quest for Responsibility*. Chapter 9.
29 Note that these two arguments in favor of the classical view do not amount to an external justification of civil servants' role obligations. The reason is the following: the obligations attached to a particular role ought to further that role's ultimate ends (Luban, David. 1988. *Lawyers and Justice: An Ethical Study*. Princeton: Princeton University Press. 128–9). If we agree that ensuring democratic accountability and guaranteeing the rule of law are among the ultimate ends of the role "civil servant of a reasonably just society," then the question becomes "How ought we to understand civil servants' role responsibility so that the role's chief aims are best realized?" The classical view suggests that these aims are best served by viewing civil servants' chief role responsibility to lie in obedience. This is not an external justification of the obligation in question, as the justification of the obligation is not independent of the role prescribing the obligation; instead, the obligation is internally related to and follows directly from the role's central objectives.
30 For a particularly forceful formulation of this position, see Brownlee. *Conscience and Conviction*.
31 Hardimon. *Role Obligations*. 344; Luban. *Lawyers and Justice*. Chapter 7.
32 Here, a critic (e.g., Wueste. *Role Moralities*. 410ff.) might object that what seems to follow from this argument is that role obligations do not, in fact, derive their normative force from the role itself, but rather from the external moral principles that justify the role. Yet, this inference is mistaken. We may concede that institutional roles and their obligations exist within a wider normative context, which includes other, external moral rules. These rules, as John Horton points out, "may set various limits to the moral obligations to which institutions can legitimately give rise, but this is not to justify those institutions or the corresponding obligations in terms of those other moral considerations" (Horton, John. 1992. *Political Obligation*. New York: Palgrave Macmillan. 157). In other words, the fact that external moral considerations place limits on role obligations does not mean that the various obligations a particular role gives rise to are *justified* by those external moral considerations rather than by the role itself.
33 Bovens. *Quest for Responsibility*. 149.
34 Of course, what constitutes "a grave threat to the public interest" will often be a matter of dispute. To some, the NSA's mass surveillance programs constitute grave government wrongdoing as they violate our rights to privacy; to others, such programs are necessary tools for securing public safety. The prospective whistleblower ought to take such disagreement into account when deciding whether or not to render certain classified information public. I further discuss the thorny concept of the public interest in Chapter 3.
35 In the case of subcontractors working for the government, however, the picture becomes more complicated. Edward Snowden, for example, was not, at the time of his disclosures, a civil servant but rather an employee of Booz Allen Hamilton. As such an employee, his main role obligation was not to the democratic constitutional state, but rather to his employer, which has a clear interest in employees not disclosing classified information, as it earns the trust of its clients

by protecting the information they provide. Accordingly, one of the primary role obligations for an employee of such a company is to refrain from whistleblowing (Booz Allen Hamilton. 2016. *Green Book: The Booz Allen Hamilton Code of Business Ethics and Conduct.* Available at: http://www.boozallen.com/content/dam/boozallen/documents/inv/boozallen-code-of-ethics.pdf. 27). In cases like Snowden's, we might thus have to address a genuine *conflict* between obligations, that is, between a complicity-based obligation to blow the whistle (to be discussed in Chapter 6) and a role obligation to remain silent. I thank Kimberley Brownlee for pressing me on this point.

36 For now, I am only concerned with the question whether such disobedience is *permitted* (despite the *pro tanto* role obligation to obey). Whether whistleblowing can ever be *obligatory* is explored in Chapter 6.

37 Kant. *Metaphysics of Morals.* Ak 6: 263.

38 Ibid. Ak 6: 257.

39 Ibid. Ak 6: 312.

40 Kant, Immanuel. 1996. On the Common Saying: That May Be True in Theory, But It Is of No Use in Practice. In *Practical Philosophy.* Ed. Mary Gregor, Trans. Mary Gregor, 277–309. Cambridge: Cambridge University Press. Ak 8: 295.

41 Kant. *Metaphysics of Morals.* Ak 6: 314.

42 Stilz, Anna. 2009. *Liberal Loyalty: Freedom, Obligation, and the State.* Princeton: Princeton University Press. 50. A similar justification of authority that does not explicitly self-identify as Kantian can be found in the work of Thomas Christiano: Christiano, Thomas. 2008. *The Constitution of Equality: Democratic Authority and its Limits.* Oxford: Oxford University Press. Chapter 6.

43 Sagar. *Secrets and Leaks.* 114.

3 The public interest and the justification of whistleblowing[1]

In the previous chapter we saw why whistleblowing is a *pro tanto* morally wrongful act. The present chapter will expound the conditions that are to be met if a particular act of whistleblowing is to be nonetheless justified. So how can whistleblowing be justified? One of the most common answers to this question – one to which the author subscribes – is that the violation of one's *pro tanto* obligation to refrain from whistleblowing can be justified if the information disclosed serves the public interest. Political philosophers,[2] legal[3] and public administration[4] scholars, whistleblower protection laws,[5] national[6] and international[7] guidance documents, and courts[8] – all agree that a breach of state secrecy by disclosing classified documents is justified if it serves the public interest. None of them, however, provide a definition of what the public interest exactly *is* nor do they explain how we may *determine* it; at the most, an *ad hoc* list of offenses is drawn up, the disclosure of which would be in the public interest.

This is problematic, because it leaves potential whistleblowers unable to ascertain whether their unauthorized disclosures will be considered justified, leading many to err on the side of caution and remain silent, depriving the public of much-needed information. Failing an agreed upon definition of the public interest or a process to determine it, a public interest *defense* of whistleblowing (to be developed in Chapter 5) also becomes problematic, as it is then up to the judges to determine whether a particular disclosure is in the public interest. This, predictably, has led to the critique that applications of the public interest in whistleblowing cases are *ad hoc*[9] and demonstrate "judicial idiosyncrasy."[10]

For these reasons, this chapter, in developing a justification of whistleblowing, will first provide some clarity concerning the public interest. Accordingly, the chapter will be structured as follows: Section 3.1 will give an overview of three common understandings of the public interest (aggregative, procedural, and unitary) and explain why they are problematic. Subsequently, Section 3.2 presents a more promising alternative, namely the civic account of the public interest, which I will defend. In brief, it argues that public interests are those interests that we all share in our role as members of the public. Finally, in addition to the public interest condition developed in Section 3.2, Section 3.3 will identify two *procedural* conditions that are to be met if a particular act of whistleblowing is to be fully justified.

3.1 Three common theories of the public interest

Though appeals to the public interest are incredibly common – in law, politics, and in ordinary speech – they are also made rather casually. As a consequence, what is meant by "the public interest" typically remains unclear. Some have held that this lack of clarity is a necessary characteristic of the concept, dismissing it altogether as vacuous.[11] Others consider the concept a convenient tool for the powerful to present their own factional interests as public interests.[12] Furthermore, some wonder whether the concept, which appears to presuppose an interest common to all, can be of any use in contemporary pluralistic societies.[13] Finally, critics worry that the concept may be abused by demagogues demanding individual sacrifices for the greater common good.[14] Because of these concerns, the concept has largely fallen out of fashion in legal and political philosophy in recent decades. As a consequence, the concept has retained its problematic protean nature, being used differently by different people in different contexts. This section will discuss the three main public interest theories: the aggregative, the procedural, and the unitary theories.[15] Each of these, however, has serious drawbacks, prompting me to sketch a more promising account in Section 3.2.

3.1.1 The aggregative account

According to Jeremy Bentham, a community consists simply of the aggregate of its members. It follows that that the "interest of the community then is, what? – the sum of the interests of the several members who compose it."[16] This is also referred to as Bentham's "compositionalism."[17] Whether a particular action, policy, or law is conducive to one's interest depends on its *utility*: "that property in any object, whereby it tends to produce benefit, advantage, pleasure, good, or happiness … or (what comes again to the same thing) to prevent the happening of mischief, pain, evil, or unhappiness to the party whose interest is considered."[18] The question whether a particular law or policy is in the public interest thus comes down to determining its effects on the happiness or welfare of each of the individual members that together constitute the public and tallying the results. If, on balance, the law or policy benefits more individuals than are harmed by it, this will demonstrate the "general *good tendency* of the act, with respect to the total number or community of individuals concerned."[19]

It follows that there is no distinct "public" with its own interests separate from the private interests of the sundry individuals that together make up the public. Rather, the public interest is determined simply by aggregating the private interests of the individual members of the public; if a policy is in the private interest of the majority of those individuals, then it is in the public interest.

The problem with this view is that we often want to distinguish between majority interests and the public interest. This concern points toward the idea that the public interest is a *moral* concept. As such, it cannot be derived from the empirical observation that the interests of some individuals outnumber the interests of others. When we ask "Is *x* in the public interest?" we want to know something other than whether *x* is in the interest of the majority. Furthermore, the aggregative method of determining the public interest may be considered morally objectionable in that it appears to render minority interests inferior to majority interests, irrespective of the content of those interests.

Finally, there is the familiar problem posed by social choice theory, namely that when voters have to make a choice between three or more alternatives (*A*, *B*, and *C*), there is no fair and rational way to determine which of these is preferred by a majority, that is, to convert voters' preferences into a social decision.[20] In its simplest form, Kenneth Arrow's impossibility theorem, which demonstrates this problem, is as follows: suppose three people – Mary, Michael, and Molly – are to rate three alternatives (e.g., policy proposals or political candidates). The following matrix shows their individual preferences:

	A	*B*	*C*
Mary	1	2	3
Michael	3	1	2
Molly	2	3	1

The matrix shows that a majority prefers *A* to *B* (Mary and Molly) and *B* to *C* (Mary and Michael). It would logically follow that a majority therefore also prefers *A* to *C*. Yet, as we can see, a majority in fact prefers *C* to *A* (Michael and Molly). From this matrix, one could thus both infer that a majority prefers *A* to *C* and that a majority prefers *C* to *A*, which is quite impossible. Next to the moral objections to the aggregative theory mentioned above, there is thus also the problem of the logical impossibility of distilling a collective ordering of preferences from the aggregate of individual preferences.

3.1.2 The procedural account

The procedural account holds that the public interest coincides with the result of a democratic decision-making procedure. The latter can be interpreted either in a pluralist or in a more deliberative manner. In an ideal pluralist scheme, democratic politics consists of a fair contest between interest groups, each seeking to influence the political agenda at the expense of others. Individuals and interest groups are focused on promoting their own self- or group interest, and whatever is the result of this contest for political influence – which must be ensured to be fair, i.e., all interests ought to receive equal consideration[21] – is the public interest. Thus, as in the aggregative account, the public interest is distilled from private interests, but the manner in which private interests lead to the public interest is different: it is not a matter of calculus, as it were, but rather of democratic competition.

The question is, however, whether such a profusion of competing private interests can ever lead to a genuinely *public* interest or must instead remain, to speak with Rousseau, "nothing but a sum of particular wills."[22] Such concerns might lead us to adopt instead a deliberative democratic approach to the public interest. Deliberative democrats argue that political debate ought not to be focused on private or group interests, but instead on the common good.[23] In fact, however, what they often argue, is that deliberators still start out with their own private interests, but that the deliberative process – in which one has to, among other things, give reasons for one's proposals that may also be acceptable to others – can transform those private interests in such a way that the final result of deliberation (the law or policy decided upon) will be in the public interest. Thus, according to the deliberative ideal, I cannot, for example, appeal to the desire to be wealthier come what may in defending a particular policy that will help me reach that goal. Instead, I must offer reasons that others may find convincing as well, reasons that do not hinge on my desire for affluence.[24] It is, therefore, not the case that deliberative democrats start from conceptions of the public interest rather than self-interest. Instead, as Ian O'Flynn has perceptively pointed out, "the hope is that deliberation will transform special interests into public interests."[25] The starting point, even for deliberative democrats it seems, is still a conflict of private (and group) interests.[26] The worry is, therefore, the same as with pluralist theories of democracy, namely whether they can truly deliver a *public* interest.

In addition, one might take issue with the strong procedural nature of this approach to the public interest. Benhabib, for example, argues that "what is considered in the common interest of all results from processes of collective deliberation."[27] And Cohen maintains that "the interests, aims and ideals that comprise the common good are those that survive deliberation,"[28] and that "what is good is fixed by public deliberation, and not prior to it."[29] But how can deliberative theorists claim both that deliberation ought to be focused on the public interest *and* that the public interest is the result of that very same deliberation?[30] The former claim seems to imply that the public interest exists independently of deliberation, whereas this is denied by the latter claim. In any case, if we wish to retain the public interest as a moral concept, we cannot simply equate it with the result of deliberation (or of the free and fair competition of interests), which is an empirical matter, after all. Furthermore, we can never be certain that citizens will deliberate judiciously and that the result will be satisfactory.[31] Finally, even if we assume ideal conditions for deliberation are present, and citizens exchange arguments with one another in a reasonable and charitable manner in conditions that are free and equal, then we still have no guarantee that they will agree which policy most serves the public interest.

3.1.3 The unitary account

Having discussed the two most prevalent theories of the public interest, we can see that they, though quite different, share a common problem: they both fail to sufficiently recognize that the public interest is a substantively *moral* concept that is identifiable independently both of democratic processes and of the majority interest. To avoid this problem, we may consider the straightforwardly normative *unitary theory* of the public interest, as found in the works of Aristotle, for example. As is well known, Aristotle viewed the state as a kind of partnership or association. Like any partnership, it is set up for the purpose of realizing a certain good common to all members. As it is the most encompassing of all partnerships, the good pursued by the state is the most comprehensive good.[32] The end at which the state aims – the good it strives to bring about – coincides with the end each individual ought to strive towards: "the best life, whether separately for an individual or collectively for states, is the life conjoined with virtue furnished with sufficient means for taking part in virtuous actions," that is, human flourishing (*eudaimonia*).[33] There is thus, for Aristotle, no conflict between the good of individuals and the common good of the polity as a whole.

Unitary theories of the public interest, as found in Aristotle (but also in Plato and Aquinas, for instance), do not derive the public interest from people's private interests, but rather from a comprehensive moral theory that applies equally to private and to public interests. Consequently, a law or policy cannot be in the public interest if it is not also in the interest of *all*, and it cannot truly be in the interest of a certain individual if it is not also in the public interest. In other words, there can be no justifiable conflict between individual interests and the public interest.[34] Contemporary liberals generally find this conception untenably problematic, given its predisposition to paternalism – after all, any assertion of a private interest that does not coincide with the public interest is dismissed as misguided – and its exclusion of conflicting interests. In today's diverse societies there can be no presumption of unanimity concerning individual interests, and it is therefore problematic to assume a unity between the individual and the collective good.

3.2 The civic account of the public interest

One of our concerns with the aggregative theories and the procedural theories of the public interest was that they did not yield genuinely *public* interests. In Rousseauian terms, they are concerned with the "will of all" rather than the "general will." So-called "common-interest theorists" evade this problem as they consider only those interests that are shared by all members of the public to be *public* interests. The obvious critique of this position is that such interests are bound to be extremely rare (if they exist at all), rendering the concept nearly meaningless. Even a law prohibiting (or limiting) the pollution of the air and water – one would at least expect the interests in clean air and water to be on the list of interests shared by all – may not be in everyone's interests. After all, some people profit from polluting the air and water, and the damages to their health (from breathing polluted air and drinking polluted water) may not outweigh the profits to be made from their polluting enterprises. The common-interest approach would, therefore, have to conclude that protecting the air and water is not in the public interest.[35]

This implausible conclusion seems to instantly discredit the common-interest approach. Yet, if we follow Brian Barry's account, we may still be able to circumvent this conclusion. He points out that disagreements over policy often spring from different people judging the policy from the perspective of a different "role." For example, a policy to lower the speeding limit in a particular neighborhood may be contrary to *A*'s interests as a motorist, but at the same time in *B*'s interests as a parent of small children. Depending on the role we occupy we may judge a policy differently. Such a conflict of interests can even be present within a single individual. After all, with respect to a given situation, we may have different interests as we simultaneously occupy different roles in relation to it (homeowner, parent, employee, nature lover, and so forth).

The next step of the argument is to point out that the only role we *all* occupy is that of a member of the public.[36] In determining wherein the public interest lies, we must therefore look to "those interests which people have in common *qua* members of the public."[37] Returning to our earlier example, we may acknowledge that legislation aimed at protecting the air and water from (excessive) pollution is not in the interest of some *qua* members of polluting industries. But, as members of the public, they share an interest in clean air and water with all other members. Legislation aimed at ensuring these goods is, therefore, in the public interest "in the sense that it is in everyone's interest *qua* member of the public."[38] Much like Rousseau's "citizen" who only has a general will, as opposed to the "man" who merely follows his own particular will,[39] in our capacity as member of the public we will be inclined to favor policies that are in the interest of all members of society rather than exclusively in our own private interest (*qua* industrialist, homeowner, employee, etc.).

Barry's theory of the public interest thus avoids many of the pitfalls of the rival theories discussed earlier. It does not assume a perfect unity between individual and community interests, as the unitary theory does, and can thus accommodate a multitude of different and often conflicting private interests in society, which is an advantage of the aggregative and procedural accounts. Contrary to those latter two approaches, however, the public interest identified by Barry is genuinely public. He holds that if we want to promote the public interest, we must promote interests that all share *as members of the public*, whereas the aggregative approach aims to simply maximize private interests for all as much as possible, and the procedural approach hopes to distill shared interests from the profusion of private interests through deliberation. Furthermore, Barry's approach occupies an attractive middle ground between the comprehensive moral position advocated by unitary theory and the subjectivist nature of the aggregative and procedural theories. The public interest is not simply the aggregate of private interests nor is it to be equated to the outcome of deliberation. The public interest, in Barry's account, is still a moral concept in the sense that private interests are excluded from its determination: in determining the *public* interest, we ought to pay heed only to our interests *as members of the public*. Yet, it does not presuppose wide agreement over a comprehensive moral theory as the unitary theory seems to do.

Finally, in identifying the public interest with the interests we share in our role as citizens, Barry's account coincides nicely with whistleblower legislation and guidance documents, which state that the fact that disclosure may serve the whistleblower's *private* interests, is not a sufficient (or even a necessary) reason for disclosure, as "what may serve those private interests does not necessarily serve a wider public interest," which alone can justify disclosure.[40]

Stating, with Barry, that the public interest consists of those interests we share *qua* members of the public, is a good first step, but it is not enough. For what *are* the interests we share as members of the public? Barry does not further specify this. But one thing we now know is that the public interest does not result from the sundry private interests we may have. If something (a law or policy) is in the public interest, this does not mean that it aims to realize certain private aims that specific individuals may have. If a law or policy serves the common good – a term closely related to the public interest[41] – this does not mean that the law or policy is aimed at realizing a particular conception of the good (or even various conceptions of the good) that individuals may have. It seems to me that the only interests we can reasonably be said to all share in our role as members of the public are interests in conditions that render it possible for each of us to develop and strive to realize our own values, objectives, and life plans. Or, to put it another way, if something is in the public interest, then it is instrumental for the realization of individuals' *private* interests, provided the pursuit of these interests does not reduce the ability of other members of the community to pursue theirs. This *civic account* of the public interest obviously does not deny that the private interests of individual members of the community may differ from one another and may even conflict; all it states is that the interests we share as members of the community are interests in conditions that need to be in place if all members are to be able to pursue their own interests.[42] For example, the unchecked arbitrary exercise of power by a ruler makes it very problematic to draft a life plan, let alone realize it, given that we do not know for sure that what is permissible today won't be decreed impermissible tomorrow. Hence, a shared interest in the rule of law. Similarly, without a sphere of protected free agency, both the formulation and the realization of a life plan become extremely difficult. We thus share an interest in fundamental human rights.[43] Further examples of interests we share in our capacity as members of the public include interests in legal certainty, the separation of powers, and political accountability.

Of course, this civic account of the public interest, which expands upon Barry's approach to the public interest, does not do away with all problems. In particular, it remains unclear what to do when the several interests we share as members of the public are in conflict, such as the interests in privacy and security. For now, we can say two things in reply: first, the fact that public interests may be in conflict does not demonstrate that the idea of the public interest itself is somehow incoherent. Indeed, as O'Flynn points out, "the values of freedom and equality can also conflict. But no one seriously suggests that we should give up on those values simply because of the many tensions that can arise between them."[44] Second, Barry points out that "interest" is a comparative concept: "'Being in someone's interest' is at least a triadic relationship between a person and at least two policies."[45] Thus, when we ask if a given policy proposal is in the public interest, we are asking whether it is *more* in the public interest than a given alternative. So, though there may be conflicting interests all members of the public share, it may still be possible to judge whether policy proposal x better serves the public interest than proposal y (for example, if the benefits to privacy promised by proposal x are quite large while the benefits to the conflicting interest of security[46] promised by proposal y are rather small, then it would seem proposal x is more in the public interest than proposal y).

It follows from this understanding of the public interest, that an act of whistleblowing is *justifiable* (i.e. meets the public interest condition) if and only if it is the case that the unauthorized disclosure of classified documents better serves the public interest than the alternative (continued secrecy). More specifically, an act of whistleblowing is justifiable if and only if the disclosure of the information does, on balance, more good than harm to the interest we share as members of the political community in those conditions that need to be in place if all members are to be able to pursue their own interests (e.g., the rule of law, the separation of powers, human rights). How exactly one determines the public interest in practice will be further clarified in Chapter 5, which will provide an exposition of the public interest defense for whistleblowing. For the moment, let us turn our attention to the two procedural conditions that are to be met for the act of whistleblowing to be *actually or fully justified*.[47]

3.3 Procedural conditions of justified whistleblowing

In order for an act of whistleblowing to be actually morally justified, it is not enough that the public interest condition is met. Two *procedural conditions* must be met as well. First, the whistleblower ought to exhaust all alternative channels before going public. Only when pursuing such alternatives is truly not a feasible option can the information, as a last resort, be disclosed to the public at large. In practice, this condition of *ultimum remedium* amounts to addressing the wrongdoing internally first. In this manner, those in charge have an opportunity to investigate and address the wrongdoing (including taking measures against those responsible) or to explain why no wrongdoing has in fact occurred, without immediately involving the larger public. Yet if nothing is done with one's complaint or if the internal procedure is not a realistic option (because, for example, it is controlled by those involved in the suspected wrongdoing), the next step is to go to an independent oversight body. This again allows the wrongdoing to be investigated and addressed in a confidential manner. When both these channels have been exhausted to no effect, or if the whistleblower reasonably believes that pursuing them would be futile, result in the destruction of evidence, or in reprisal against the whistleblower, or a third party, or if the information involved concerns an imminent risk or threat "to the life, health, and safety of persons, or to the environment,"[48] then the information may be disclosed to the public, preferably through an established media outlet.

The second procedural condition requires the whistleblower to take the necessary steps to *minimize the harm* her disclosures could cause. Unauthorized disclosures could, for example, have harmful consequences for individuals by publicizing the names of undercover agents. Another possibility is that national security could be harmed when the information disclosed contains military documents describing troop movements, for example, which the enemy could use to its advantage. Given these possible harms, the information to be disclosed must be diligently edited. Any information not strictly needed to address the wrongdoing in question is not to be disclosed, nor is any information that may lead to harm to particular individuals or to national security. A third possible harm that could result from whistleblowing concerns public trust in government, which will likely decline if disclosures revealing government wrongdoing become a frequent occurrence. Mere transparency of information will not necessarily inspire trustworthiness and trust (one of the main arguments in support of transparency) if the information is not correctly received by the intended audience or if the information itself is inaccurate or misleading. In fact, transparency can potentially even "worsen communication by spreading confusion, superstition, false and misleading beliefs, misinformation, and even disinformation."[49]

Given these three possible harms, whistleblowers would be well advised to collaborate with news outlets that have the experience and knowledge required to carefully edit the information so that only the information necessary for revealing wrongdoing is made public and nothing more. Furthermore, such news outlets can place the information in the right context so that the intended audience can adequately receive and understand it.

Of course, the possibility of inflicting some kind of harm through unauthorized disclosures cannot be entirely excluded, despite all the precautions taken by the whistleblower. Accordingly, this procedural condition requires the *minimization* and not the *elimination* of harm. If the whistleblower has taken the above-mentioned measures to mitigate harm from the disclosure, yet the disclosure still results in some harm to the reputations of the officials responsible for a deeply unjust, secret policy and in a decrease of public trust in government, then we must not conclude that the responsibility for this decline in trust lies with the whistleblower. Rather, it lies with the officials' decisions to execute unjust policies. Even if the information exposes the violation of human rights, significantly damaging the responsible country's reputation abroad and possibly arousing furious reactions among the victims of such unjust policies, such harm ought not to count as proof that the whistleblower has not met the minimization of harm condition. Otherwise, paradoxically, meeting this condition would become increasingly difficult "as the behavior disclosed entailed more shocking and criminal conduct."[50]

The attentive reader will have noted that I have not included a "good faith" condition, as many do.[51] As an, ideally, public-spirited breach of one's obligations, classified public whistleblowing is comparable to civil disobedience.[52] According to the standard account, civil disobedience is characterized by the public and open nature of the disobedient act. Such openness *and* the willingness to accept punishment demonstrate fidelity to law. This fidelity to law confirms to one's fellow citizens that one acted with good motives, that is, with an eye toward the public good.[53] Similarly, the reason why many scholars in the philosophical debate on whistleblowing maintain that the whistleblower ought to reveal her identity for the act of whistleblowing to be justified, is that this would enable us, the public, to judge whether she acted with the public good in mind or, rather, from selfish or partisan motives. If the latter is the case, the whistleblower might have provided only a partial or a distorted version of the truth in order to mislead the public and obtain her private or sectional goal.[54]

Regarding this question of motive, the law seems to be leaving philosophy behind. In the UK, for example, the requirement of good faith was struck from the Public Interest Disclosure Act in 2013. Instead, a disclosure now simply needs to be in the public interest.[55] The main argument against including the motive of the whistleblower as a procedural condition is that what matters is to have good *reasons*, not good *motives*. So long as the whistleblower has good *reasons* to disclose classified information – ensured by the public interest condition – their less than perfect motives become irrelevant for the justifiability of the act. If the disclosed information contains evidence of grave government wrongdoing threatening the public interest, then disclosure is justifiable (as it better serves the public interest than continued secrecy). The whistleblower's possibly base motive does not change this. Disclosing Watergate, for example, was certainly in the public interest, even though personal resentment (over having been passed over for promotion) may also have played a role. We ought to, therefore, discount the motive and focus instead on the reasons for disclosure, that is, on the *content* of the information. The public interest condition combined with the two procedural conditions will need to suffice to prevent the abuse that worries the advocates of the good faith condition. Finally, it must be noted that the condition of a genuine ethical conviction is no guarantee for the exclusion of undesirable acts of whistleblowing, as the following apposite remark by Jürgen Habermas compellingly illustrates: "the legitimacy of acts of resistance cannot simply be deduced from the ethical seriousness of the actor's motives. It was hardly a failing of conscience that separated Ulrike Meinhoff from Sophie Scholl."[56]

Finally, a remark must be made concerning the hierarchy of the justifying conditions. The three conditions do not carry equal weight. Rather, the public interest condition is a *threshold condition*. In other words, if the public interest condition is not met, the whole process of assessing the justifiability of a concrete case of whistleblowing ends immediately. Viewing the public interest condition as a threshold condition in this manner indicates its preponderance over the two procedural conditions. This is reflective of the fact that civil servants do not blow the whistle in order to minimize harm or to verify the authenticity of documents. Instead, they do so in order to serve the public interest by unveiling grave government wrongdoing.

The function of this distinction between the threshold condition and the two procedural conditions is to allow us to assess concrete cases of whistleblowing in a more precise and subtle fashion. Specifically, the wrongfulness or justness of whistleblowing thus becomes a matter of degree. In order to demonstrate this, let us first take another look at the three conditions of justified whistleblowing:

> *Threshold condition (TC)*
> The information disclosed must serve the public interest.
>
> *Procedural condition 1 (PC1)*
> One ought to exhaust alternative, more discreet channels for disclosure.
>
> *Procedural condition 2 (PC2)*
> One ought to take steps to minimize the harm caused by the disclosure of the information.

Depending on which (if any) conditions are met, we may deem a concrete case of classified public whistleblowing more or less justified or wrongful. The following options seem exhaustive:

1. *Simply wrong*: none of the conditions are met.
2. *Faux-whistleblowing*: PC1 and PC2 are both met, but TC is not. Justified whistleblowing ought to be limited to the addressing of grave wrongdoing that is of public interest. If the information does not concern such wrongdoing, the unauthorized disclosure has not met the threshold condition and is, therefore, not justifiable. The disclosure of classified information that does not serve the public interest is wrongful, even if PC1 and PC2 have been met, though less so than the first option, as an attempt has at least been made to minimize harm.[57]

3. *Justifiable but not actually or fully justified*: TC is met, but either PC1 or PC2, or both, are not met. This is a justifiable case of whistleblowing, but executed in the wrong manner, and thus still wrong, but significantly less so than the first two options, given that the threshold condition has been met.

4. *Justified*: all the conditions are met. The act of whistleblowing is fully justified.

These four possibilities show that there are gradations of wrongfulness (and justifiability); it is not a simple matter of right or wrong. The distinction between TC and the PCs means that the most weight should be accorded to the question whether the disclosure serves the public interest (typically by revealing grave government wrongdoing). Consequently, options 1 and 2 are by far more wrongful than options 3 and 4. Being able to distinguish various gradations of moral wrongfulness could be important when considering the legal consequences of (more or less) wrongful cases of whistleblowing (as will become apparent in Chapter 5).

3.4 Conclusion

This chapter has undertaken to clarify what is generally regarded as the most fundamental condition for justified whistleblowing, namely that it be in the public interest. According to the civic account of the public interest defended here, the public interest consists of interests we share in our role as members of the community. Those interests were further identified as interests in conditions that render it possible for each of us to develop and strive to realize our own values, objectives, and life plans. Examples of such conditions include political accountability, human rights, and the rule of law. It follows from this understanding of the public interest, that an act of whistleblowing meets the public interest condition if and only if it is the case that the unauthorized disclosure of classified documents better serves the public interest than the alternative (i.e., continued secrecy). More specifically, an act of whistleblowing is justifiable if and only if the disclosure of the information did, on balance, more good than harm to the interest we share as members of the political community in those conditions that need to be in place if all members are to be able to pursue their own interests.

In addition to the public interest condition, I have identified two procedural conditions: the exhaustion of legal alternatives (*ultimum remedium*) and the minimization of harm. Finally, I have pointed out that these three conditions do not stand on an equal footing: the public interest condition is a threshold condition, indicating its greater importance with respect to the two procedural conditions. This distinction between the public interest condition and the procedural conditions will allow us to distinguish between varying degrees of either wrongful or justifiable whistleblowing.

Having provided a conceptual clarification of the public interest as well as an exposition of the conditions for justified whistleblowing, it remains for us to see how both of these can be applied to actual cases of unauthorized disclosures. This task will be undertaken in Chapter 5, which will present a public interest defense of whistleblowing. First, however, the next chapter will discuss the most commonly proposed defense for justified cases of whistleblowing, namely the defense based on individual rights (typically the right to freedom of expression).

Notes

1 This chapter draws from Boot, Eric R. 2019. The Feasibility of a Public Interest Defense for Whistleblowing. *Law and Philosophy*. Forthcoming. It also draws from Boot, Eric R. 2017. Classified Public Whistleblowing: how to Justify a *pro tanto* Wrong. *Social Theory and Practice* 43: 541–67.

2 Bok, Sissela. 1984. *Secrets: On the Ethics of Concealment and Revelation*. New York: Vintage Books. 219; Delmas, Candice. 2014. The Civic Duty to Report Crime and Corruption. *Les ateliers de l'éthique* 9: 50–64. 62; Kumar, Manohar, and Daniele Santoro. 2017. A Justification of Whistleblowing. *Philosophy and Social Criticism* 43: 669–84. 676ff.; Sagar, Rahul. 2013. *Secrets and Leaks: The Dilemma of State Secrecy*. Princeton: Princeton University Press. 13.

3 Benkler, Yochai. 2014. A Public Accountability Defense for National Security Leakers and Whistleblowers. *Harvard Law and Policy Review* 8: 281–326; Kagiaros, Dimitrios. 2015. Protecting "National Security" Whistleblowers in the Council of Europe: An Evaluation of Three Approaches on How to Balance National Security with Freedom of Expression. *The International Journal of Human Rights* 19: 408–28.

4 Bovens, Mark. 1998. The Quest for Responsibility: Accountability and Citizenship in Complex Organisations. Cambridge: Cambridge University Press. 163ff.

5 The UK *Public Interest Disclosure Act*; the Dutch *Wet huis voor klokkenluiders* (*House for Whistleblowers Act*), Article 1(d).

6 UK Information Commissioner's Office. 2016. *The Public Interest Test: Freedom of Information Act*. Retrieved from: https://ico.org.uk/media/for-organisations/documents/1183/the_public_interest_test.pdf.

7 Open Society Foundations. 2013. *The Global Principles on National Security and the Right to Information (Tshwane Principles)*. Available at: https://www.opensocietyfoundations.org/publications/global-principles-national-security-and-freedom-information-tshwane-principles. Principle 37.

8 E.g., European Court of Human Rights (ECtHR) (Grand Chamber). *Guja v. Moldova*. 12 February 2008. Application No. 14277/04. § 74. Specifically, the Court considered whether the public interest in upholding secrecy was strong enough to warrant a violation of the whistleblower's Article 10 right to free speech, or that, instead, the public interest in disclosure argued in favor of upholding his Article 10 right.

 9 McHarg, Aileen. 1999. Reconciling Human Rights and the Public Interest: Conceptual Problems and Doctrinal Uncertainty in the Jurisprudence of the European Court of Human Rights. *The Modern Law Review* 62: 671–96. 683.
10 Lewis, David. 2015. Is a Public Interest Test for Workplace Whistleblowing in Society's Interest? *International Journal of Law and Management* 57: 141–58. 143.
11 Schubert, Glendon. 1960. *The Public Interest*. Glencoe (Ill.): Free Press. 223–4.
12 Marx, Karl, and Friedrich Engels. 2014. Chapter One, "Feuerbach". In *"German Ideology" Manuscripts: Presentation and Analysis of the "Feuerbach Chapter."* Ed. Joseph O'Malley, Trans. Terrell Carver and Daniel Blank. New York: Palgrave. 183.
13 O'Flynn, Ian. 2010. Deliberating About the Public Interest. *Res Publica* 16: 299–315. 300.
14 Mansbridge, Jane. 1998. On the Contested Nature of the Public Good. In *Private Action and the Public Good*. Eds. Walter W. Powell and Elisabeth Stephanie Clemens, 3–19. New Haven: Yale University Press. 4.
15 For this list of categories, I am indebted to both Held (Held, Virginia. 1970. *The Public Interest and Individual Interests*. New York: Basic Books. 42–6) and Mansbridge (Mansbridge. *Public Good*. 9–11), though I depart from both of their lists of categories at times.
16 Bentham, Jeremy. 1996. *An Introduction to the Principles of Morals and Legislation*. Eds. J.H. Burns and H.L.A. Hart. Oxford: Oxford University Press. 12.
17 Postema, Gerald J. 2006. Interests, Universal and Particular: Bentham's Utilitarian Theory of Value. *Utilitas* 18: 109–33. 111.
18 Bentham. *An Introduction*. 12.
19 Ibid. 40.
20 See, e.g., Arrow, Kenneth J. 1963. *Social Choice and Individual Values*. 2nd ed. New Haven: Yale University Press.
21 Dahl, Robert A. 1989. *Democracy and Its Critics*. New Haven: Yale University Press. 297.
22 Rousseau, Jean-Jacques. 1997. Of the Social Contract. In *The Social Contract and Other Later Political Writings*. Ed. Victor Gourevitch, Trans. Victor Gourevitch, 39–152. Cambridge: Cambridge University Press. Bk. II, Ch. 3 [2].
23 See, e.g., Cohen, Joshua. 1989. Deliberation and Democratic Legitimacy. In *The Good Polity: Normative Analysis of the State*. Eds. Alan Hamlin and Philip Pettit, 17–34. Oxford: Basil Blackwell.
24 Ibid. 24.
25 O'Flynn. *Deliberating*. 308.
26 See, e.g., Benhabib, Seyla. 1996. Toward a Deliberative Model of Democratic Legitimacy. In *Democracy and Difference: Contesting the Boundaries of the Political*. Ed. Seyla Benhabib, 67–94. Princeton: Princeton University Press. 73: "the deliberative model of democracy proceeds not only from a conflict of values but also from a conflict of interests in social life." Also see Mansbridge, Jane, James Bohman, Simone Chambers, David Estlund, Andreas Føllesdal, Archon Fung, Cristina Lafont, Bernard Manin, and José Luis Martí. 2010. The Place of Self-Interest and the Role of Power in Deliberative Democracy. *Journal of Political Philosophy* 18: 64–100, in which a number of prominent deliberative democratic theorists argue for a greater role of self-interest in democratic deliberation.
27 Benhabib. *Toward a Deliberative Model*. 69.
28 Cohen. *Deliberation*. 25.

29 Ibid. 29; cf. Calhoun, Craig. 1998. The Public as a Social and Cultural Project. In *Private Action and the Public Good*. Eds. Walter W. Powell and Elisabeth Stephanie Clemens, 20–35. New Haven: Yale University Press. 32.
30 O'Flynn. *Deliberating*. 302.
31 Ibid. 308.
32 Aristotle. 1944. *Politics*. Translated by H. Rackham. Cambridge (Mass.): Harvard University Press. I.i 1252a1–6.
33 Ibid. VII.i 1323b40–1324a2. Cf. VII.ii 1324a5–8: "On the other hand it remains to say whether the happiness of a state is to be pronounced the same as that of each individual man, or whether it is different. Here too the answer is clear: everybody would agree that it is the same."
34 Held. *Public Interest*. 136.
35 Goodin, Robert E. 1996. Institutionalizing the Public Interest: The Defense of Deadlock and Beyond. *The American Political Science Review* 90: 331–43. 338.
36 Barry, Brian. 1964. The Public Interest. *Proceedings of the Aristotelian Society* 38: 1–18. 14–15.
37 Barry, Brian. 1965. *Political Argument*. London: Routledge & Kegan Paul. 190.
38 Ibid. 224. Note that, contrary to the unitary theory, this account of the public interest *does* allow for the possibility of *x* being contrary to my private interests but still in the public interest. There is thus no presupposed unity between public and private interests.
39 Rousseau. *The Social Contract*. Bk. I, Ch. 7 [7]. Cf. Cohen, Joshua. 2010. *Rousseau: A Free Community of Equals*. Oxford: Oxford University Press. 54: "As citizens, they are not to rely on their private will in assessing regulations or deciding whether to comply, nor are they to balance considerations of personal advantage and of the common good. Instead, they are to deliberate about what the laws should be by reference to considerations of the common good (common interests), and to deliberate about conduct by giving first consideration to reasons of the common good."
40 UK Information Commissioner's Office. *Public Interest Test*. 7.
41 Though some have argued that the public interest is more minimalist than the common good, concerning chiefly material well-being, whereas the common good also concerns people's moral character and personal development (Douglass, Bruce. 1980. The Common Good and the Public Interest. *Political Theory* 8: 103–17).
42 For this elaboration of Barry's understanding of the public interest I am indebted to John Finnis's work on the common good, which he views as synonymous with the public interest: Finnis, John. 2011. *Natural Law and Natural Rights*. 2nd ed. Oxford: Oxford University Press. Ch. 6.
43 Socioeconomic rights as well as civil and political rights. After all, a certain level of physical well-being is a necessary precondition for the possibility of pursuing one's interests and realizing one's objectives.
44 O'Flynn. *Deliberating*. 313.
45 Barry. *Political Argument*. 192.
46 Privacy and security are here to be understood as specifications of the more general public interest in human rights.
47 The terms "justifiable" and "actually justified" are used in order to express the following thought: if the public interest condition is met, the violation of duty is *justifiable*, but a concrete case of whistleblowing only becomes *actually justified* if the procedural conditions are met as well.
48 *Tshwane Principles*. Principle 40a.

49 O'Neill, Onora. 2006. Transparency and the Ethics of Communication. In *Transparency: The Key to Better Governance?* Eds. D. Heald and Ch. Hood, 75–90. Oxford: Oxford University Press. 83–4.
50 Benkler. *Public Accountability Defense.* 307.
51 See, e.g., Bok, Sissela. 1984. *Secrets: On the Ethics of Concealment and Revelation.* New York: Vintage Books. 223; ECtHR. *Guja v. Moldova.* § 77; Sagar. *Secrets and Leaks.* 134–5.
52 This is not to say they are equivalent, as we will see in the next chapter.
53 Rawls, John. 1999. *A Theory of Justice.* Revised ed. Cambridge (Mass.): Belknap Press of Harvard University Press. 322. Cf. King, Martin Luther. 1964. Letter from Birmingham Jail. In *Why We Can't Wait,* 77–100. New York: Harper and Row. 86: "One who breaks an unjust law must do so openly, lovingly, and with a willingness to accept the penalty."
54 Bok. *Secrets.* 224; Sagar. *Secrets and Leaks.* 135ff.; Jubb, Peter B. 1999. Whistleblowing: A Restrictive Definition and Interpretation. *Journal of Business Ethics* 21: 77–94. 92.
55 Ashton, Jeanette. 2015. 15 Years of Whistleblowing Protection under the Public Interest Disclosure Act 1998: Are We Still Shooting the Messenger? *Industrial Law Journal* 44: 29–52.
56 Habermas, Jürgen. 1985. Civil Disobedience: Litmus Test for the Democratic Constitutional State. *Berkeley Journal of Sociology* 30: 95–116. 105.
57 Incidentally, this does not seem a likely option. Going through the normal channels of addressing wrongdoing first before going public will most likely filter out all disclosures of information that is not of public concern.

4 Possible legal defenses for justified whistleblowing (1)

A right to whistleblowing?[1]

In the previous chapter, we have seen how classified public whistleblowing can be morally justified. The question that concerns me in this chapter and the next is what form a legal defense of justified whistleblowing should take. The main claim will be that a legal defense of whistleblowing cannot be based on individual *rights*, be they legal or moral, though this is indeed a very commonly proposed defense. Proponents of a legal rights-based defense of whistleblowing argue that the legal right to freedom of expression – understood broadly as a right to seek, receive, use, and impart information – covers acts of whistleblowing (provided certain conditions are met). Section 4.1 argues against such an individual legal rights-based defense of whistleblowing, because, first, there can be no such thing as a legal right to break the law; second, the conception of rights involved in the defense deviates significantly (and unappealingly) from the common understanding of rights; and third, the individual rights-based defense does not do justice to the fact that the value of unauthorized disclosures lies in their *public* importance rather than in individual liberty; the defense ought to, therefore, not be based on *individual* rights but on the *public* role of whistleblowers.

Perhaps, however, there might be a *moral* right to classified public whistleblowing. Section 4.2 considers whether David Lefkowitz's argument for a moral right to civil disobedience can be applied to the case of classified public whistleblowing. Ultimately, I will conclude that it cannot, given the significant differences between civil disobedience and whistleblowing. In particular, I will argue that the degree of wrongdoing involved in wrongful exercises of a supposed moral right to whistleblowing forces us to reject such a right. If we wish to provide whistleblowers with a measure of protection we must therefore look elsewhere.

4.1 Problems with the individual legal rights-based defense

The existence of whistleblower protection legislation in many countries shows us that individuals have a legal right to engage in internal whistleblowing (whereby the reporting of wrongdoing is done within the organization) and external whistleblowing through the appropriate supervisory bodies. When it comes to disclosing state secrets to the public, however, whistleblower protection legislation as well as international standards are either considerably less clear, or they outright exclude any legal protection for those who make such disclosures. As mentioned in Chapter 1, the 2016 general Dutch whistleblower protection law states that whether disclosures to the media are protected will need to be decided on a case-by-case basis.[2] By contrast, the UK's *Official Secrets Act*, for example, flatly denies (former) members of the security services a right, "even as a last resort and even in the face of the most serious iniquity, to make a general disclosure."[3] Similarly, in the United States, federal government employees in general, let alone whistleblowers from the intelligence community, are not protected from retaliation if the information disclosed had been properly classified.[4] There is thus no separate legal right to engage in what I have termed "classified public whistleblowing" in any of the above-mentioned countries.[5] Nonetheless, in order to attempt to protect whistleblowers from retaliation, lawyers and legal scholars tend to argue that unauthorized disclosures may enjoy protection under the right to freedom of expression. Accordingly, whenever a whistleblowing case has been brought before the European Court of Human Rights, the defendant has claimed that the state has violated their Article 10 right to freedom of expression. Similarly, in the American context, defendants may appeal based on their First Amendment rights.[6] Proponents of a right to whistleblowing being included in the right to freedom of expression construe the latter broadly as a "right to seek, receive, use, and impart information."[7] Sanctions against whistleblowers are, consequently, described as violations of *rights*, provided certain conditions are met.[8]

This appears to be the most straightforward defense of whistleblowing. It is also an extremely appealing defense, as the importance of free speech in democratic societies is generally recognized: without the free flow of information, public debate would be impoverished and political accountability impaired. Despite the apparent appeal of this defense, however, I will argue that an individual legal rights-based defense of whistleblowing has some serious conceptual and practical difficulties and must, therefore, be rejected.

First, how does one reconcile the statement "There is a legal right to classified public whistleblowing" with the general prohibition of such whistleblowing? Assuming that the proponents of a right to whistleblowing (subsumed under the right to freedom of expression) accept that there is such a thing as legitimate state secrecy and that, therefore, the disclosure of state secrets ought to be (generally) prohibited, a general right to unauthorized disclosures, on the basis of which the whistleblower would enjoy legal protection, is extremely problematic. Once again, assuming that the unauthorized disclosure of state secrets ought to be illegal, a legally recognized right to whistleblowing would amount to the law recognizing a right to deliberately break the law. Even the staunchest defenders of civil disobedience have been forced by similar concerns to deny that there is such a thing as a legal right to civil disobedience,[9] and I cannot see why we ought to conclude any differently in the case of whistleblowing.

Second, the manner in which the individual rights-based defense is usually set up already shows that a possible right to whistleblowing would in no way be a right as we ordinarily understand it. For example, the European Court of Human Rights, in its first case dealing with classified public whistleblowing, maintained that, in order to ascertain whether an unauthorized disclosure will enjoy protection under the right to freedom of expression, the harm suffered by the public authority as a result of the disclosure may not outweigh "the interest of the public in having the information revealed."[10] In other words, the Court argued that if we wish to determine whether a particular restriction of the right to freedom of expression is proportionate, we need to weigh the harm inflicted by the disclosure upon the public authority against the interest of the public in receiving the information involved. Similarly, the *Tshwane Principles on National Security and the Right to Information* wish to provide whistleblowers some legal protection by appealing to a general right to information (which includes a right to free expression), but ultimately the authors frame their defense of unauthorized disclosures in terms of a balancing exercise between two public interests:[11] "the law should provide a public interest defense if the public interest in disclosure of the information in question outweighs the public interest in nondisclosure."[12]

In these two characteristic examples one can see the language employed drifting away from individual rights and toward public interests. To be sure, many rights, including the right to freedom of expression, contain provisions limiting their scope in order to account for the rights of others, public health, national security, and the like. Usually, however, these other interests are weighed against the right in question. For example, with hate speech the importance of the individual's ability to freely exercise their right to freedom of expression is weighed against the rights of others and public safety, among other things. The proposed defense of whistleblowing, however, is different. Here the decision whether an act of whistleblowing ought to enjoy legal protection depends on the outcome of a balancing exercise, weighing the public interest in disclosure against the public interest in nondisclosure. The difference is that in the latter case the whistleblower's supposed right to disclose classified information (subsumed under the right to freedom of expression) does not enter the equation, and is apparently appealed to for mere rhetorical purposes. Furthermore, though the right to freedom of expression is indeed subject to the above-mentioned limiting provisions, its structure still differs fundamentally from that of the proposed right to unauthorized disclosures: the former right *always* allows one to express oneself as one wishes, except in a few limiting cases (which, furthermore, "must be narrowly interpreted and the necessity for any restrictions must be convincingly established"[13]); by contrast, the latter right *never* allows the behavior the right supposedly protects (i.e., unauthorized disclosures), except if specific conditions are met.

The legal rights-based defense of whistleblowing thus appeals to a right to whistleblowing, yet this supposed right apparently plays no (or a negligible) role in the balancing exercise that is to decide whether a particular unauthorized disclosure ought to be protected by that right. Clearly, this approach to a defense based on legal rights involves a notion of rights that deviates significantly from how we habitually understand them. The function of rights is to ensure a sphere of autonomous action for the right-holder. Accordingly, my right to x imposes a correlative duty on all others (in the case of universal rights like the right to freedom of expression) not to interfere with my exercise of this right. To state, then, that whether or not I will be allowed to exercise my right to x depends on the outcome of an intricate balancing exercise whereby various public interests are weighed against each other, is essentially to state that I do not have the right to x. We need not even go as far as Dworkin and state that rights must always trump all other interests, such as general welfare, national security, or public health.[14] Most scholars agree, however, that one typical characteristic of rights (certainly of fundamental rights) is their *peremptory force*:[15] the assertion of a right is not just another consideration to take into account, but a particularly weighty one that, in principle, cuts off further debate concerning what is to be done. All the more puzzling (and somewhat ironic) then that, instead of asserting at least the *prima facie* peremptory force of the right to whistleblowing, human rights lawyers and scholars (of all people) are proposing a right to whistleblowing, the enjoyment of which depends on an intricate process of balancing multiple interests, whereby the right itself plays no role of any significance. In this manner, the peremptory force that sets rights apart in normative discourse is lost.

A third and final point is that basing a defense of whistleblowing on individual rights misrepresents our reasons for wishing to protect whistleblowers. The reason is not that engaging in unauthorized disclosures constitutes a fundamental interest all people have and that, therefore, ought to be protected (as is the case with fundamental rights). Rather, the reason is that unauthorized disclosures are often our main source for finding out about government wrongdoing. As Yochai Benkler puts it: "The defense [of whistleblowing] is premised on the proposition that the leaker serves a public role, so the defense [ought to be] public and systemic, rather than individual-rights based."[16] An individual legal rights-based defense does not, therefore, accurately explain the importance of whistleblowing, and it misrepresents our reasons for wishing to offer justified cases of whistleblowing some protection.

4.2 No moral right to classified public whistleblowing

Having ruled out a defense based on a *legal* right to whistleblowing, we might consider the possibility of a *moral* right to whistleblowing. Given that we ordinarily assume that it must be possible for a moral right to become a legal right,[17] and given that there can be no legal right to break the law, it seems there can also be no moral right to whistleblowing. Some scholars, however, have contested this "legal-right presumption," arguing for the existence of certain moral rights despite the fact that they cannot be translated into legal rights.[18] Though it may not provide much of an actual defense to whistleblowers, let us nonetheless explore this option. I will do so as follows: I will start by assuming that for there to be a moral right to whistleblowing it must at least not be morally wrongful. Subsequently, I will give two reasons why the act of whistleblowing constitutes a *pro tanto* wrong, leading me to conclude that, therefore, there cannot be a moral right to whistleblowing. Perhaps, however, one could avoid this conclusion by positing a moral right to do wrong. In considering this possibility, I begin by expounding the argument for such a right in general, after which I offer some points of criticism, which render it problematic. Putting these worries aside, however, I will next consider whether specifically the defense of civil disobedience based on a moral right to do wrong, as expounded by David Lefkowitz, can be used to argue for a moral right to classified public whistleblowing. I will argue that, given significant differences between civil disobedience and whistleblowing, it cannot.

4.2.1 Classified public whistleblowing as a pro tanto wrong

Presumably, for there to be a moral right to whistleblowing, the act of whistleblowing must be either morally obligatory or morally permissible, but not morally wrongful. However, as we have seen in Chapter 2, classified public whistleblowing does not meet this condition as it constitutes a *pro tanto* wrongful act for two reasons: it involves a breach of (1) promissory obligations and (2) the obligation to respect the democratic allocation of power.[19] Regarding the first reason, recall that civil servants are often made to swear an oath stating that they will refrain from disclosing classified documents that they encounter in the course of their work. Unauthorized disclosures constitute a violation of this promissory obligation and are therefore *pro tanto* wrongful. Naturally, to say that promise-making has normative consequences is not to say that one could simply promise to do anything, however reprehensible, and be considered under obligation to keep one's promise, even if to do so would involve grave wrongdoing. I am not bound to kill an innocent child just because, to quote Lady Macbeth, "I had so sworn." There is, however, a significant difference between promising to do a by definition immoral act (say, killing an innocent person) and promising to respect the classified nature of certain government documents. The latter promise does not, in principle, bind one to perform morally reprehensible acts, particularly if one presupposes nearly just conditions, as I do.

Second, the obligation to respect the democratic allocation of power prohibits civil servants from whistleblowing. The thought is that whistleblowers usurp the power to decide what is and what is not a legitimate state secret, whereas this is properly the prerogative of our democratically elected officials. These officials have received a mandate from the people to, among many other things, decide upon matters of state secrecy, whereas those engaged in whistleblowing have been elected neither by the people nor by its representatives.

4.2.2 A moral right to do wrong?

Despite the fact that these are *pro tanto* obligations – which are liable to be defeated by weightier moral reasons, possibly rendering a particular act of whistleblowing justified – they do establish the *pro tanto* wrongfulness of whistleblowing. As a consequence, arguing that there ought to, nonetheless, be a moral right to whistleblowing seems to be ruled out, as we would, in effect, be proposing a moral right to perform morally wrongful acts. However, there are those who argue for precisely such a right, that is, a right to do wrong. They do so on the basis of what they perceive to be the function of rights. The thought is that a right has nothing to say about the moral value of this or that action; all it does, is protect decision-making in a particular area, in which the agent is to be safe from interference: "to protect decision making is not to provide a reason for the making of any particular decision."[20] It follows that one has a right[21] to participate in morally wrongful behavior: one thus has a right to participate in a demonstration in support of a political party with openly racist views; one has a right to donate nothing to charity though one has the means to do so; one has a right to deliberately provide false information to hapless strangers asking for directions. Having a moral right in these cases does not imply any judgment concerning the moral worth (or lack thereof rather) of the actions protected by the right; it merely ensures protection from interference in a particular sphere of action.

According to its proponents, the moral right to do wrong is of great importance because without it we would not be able to make truly autonomous choices; we would not, in other words, be able to freely determine the course of our life and the content of our character. If our rights only grant us protection from interference with rightful conduct, then we are no longer able to make meaningful choices in life. Making morally sensitive choices is central to our self-constitution; they play a large part in determining who we are. And if we are not free to make morally wrong decisions, but may instead only perform morally obligatory and permissible acts, then the scope of our freedom of choice is greatly restricted, essentially robbing us of any meaningful choice at all.[22] As Jeremy Waldron puts it, rights would then only protect free choice in those areas of conduct that concern the "banalities and trivia of human life."[23]

There are, however, serious worries about this supposed moral right to do wrong, especially concerning the value of autonomous wrongdoing. Autonomy, according to the advocates of such a right, resides in the unimpeded freedom to choose to act however one wishes, whether one chooses morally right or morally wrongful actions. Therefore, if one's freedom to choose is reduced to actions that are morally required or merely permissible, the scope of one's freedom of choice is diminished, resulting in a loss of autonomy. Yet, one might argue that autonomously choosing to perform a wrongful act is an oxymoron, as it was for Kant. Autonomy, for him, resides in obeying our own lawgiving will, which, ideally, is synonymous with the moral law. An immoral act can thus *per definitionem* not be an autonomous act.[24] If, however, one finds Kant's rather thick understanding of autonomy unappealing, one may point out, with Raz, that "autonomy is *valuable* only if exercised in pursuit of the good."[25] It follows that, though wrongful acts may still be viewed as autonomous, they lack any value. Indeed, one might go further and argue that autonomously choosing to do wrong is morally worse than doing so non-autonomously. If this is the case – if autonomous wrongdoing has no, or even worse, a negative moral value – then what reason could we possibly have for advocating a right to do wrong? Or, as Raz puts it: "Since autonomy is valuable only if it is directed at the good it supplies no reason to provide, nor any reason to protect, worthless let alone bad options."[26]

Furthermore, one could reply to the proponents of a right to do wrong that, contrary to what they claim, choosing among morally permissible actions includes a great many relevant choices.[27] Think of choosing a faith, a political party, a profession, a life partner. These are choices that constitute who we are. They therefore by no means concern solely banalities and trivialities.

4.2.3   Civil disobedience and the right to do wrong

But even if we were to put aside these objections and accept, for the sake of argument, the coherence of a moral right to do wrong, a moral right to whistleblowing would still remain problematic. According to their own reasoning, those who support a right to do wrong must allow whistleblowing even when it is not the right thing to do. Such a train of thought led Raz to caution proponents of a moral right to civil disobedience as follows: "Those who hold that there is a right to civil disobedience are committed to the view that in general the rightness of the cause contributes not at all to the justification of civil disobedience."[28] A right to civil disobedience would thus entitle one to disobey even when one ought not to. Proponents of a moral right to civil disobedience, however, have bitten the bullet and affirmed that even if an agent engages in civil disobedience with the aim of substituting a just law with a law she deems more just but is actually worse (from the standpoint of justice), she still acts within her moral rights.[29] Let us consider one such argument, put forward by David Lefkowitz.

His reasoning is as follows: though I may recognize others' political beliefs to be reasonable, I can still conclude that they are erroneous. I cannot, however (nor can society as a whole), demand from them that they refrain from advocating their reasonable but wrong beliefs. The reason why is grounded in Rawls's concept of reasonable disagreement. Rawls maintains that "[m]any of our most important judgments are made under conditions where it is not to be expected that conscientious persons with full powers of reason, even after free discussion, will arrive at the same conclusion."[30] Given the burdens of judgment, we ought to therefore recognize the "right to advocate for the adoption in law or policy of reasonable views [people] sincerely believe to be true, even when they are not."[31] We ought to recognize, in other words, the right to do wrong in the sphere of politics. If one, instead, limits the sphere of free political agency to the promotion of ends we believe to be morally valuable, that would impede the leading of an autonomous life, one in which agents themselves decide over the direction their lives will take.

The next crucial step made by proponents of a moral right to civil disobedience is to subsume that said right under the more general right of political participation[32] or freedom of expression.[33] Lefkowitz, for example, argues that members of a position that does not obtain the majority in a vote may well be justified in feeling that if there had been more time to deliberate and if they had had more resources to help spread their message, perhaps they would have gained more support and eventually won over the majority. Acknowledgment of this fact leads us to recognize that the right to political participation not only consists of a right to vote, but also a right to continue to challenge the decision reached by a majority rule procedure, not only by means of legal forms of protest but also through civil disobedience.[34] Punishing a person for engaging in an act of civil disobedience thus demonstrates the state's lack of respect for that person as someone who has a moral right, like anyone else, to participate in the decision-making process that determines the laws and policies that regulate our collective life, even after a decision has been made. Consequently, Lefkowitz concludes that "to punish a person for engaging in public disobedience is equivalent to punishing a person for exercising the right to vote or the right to free speech."[35] Furthermore, given reasonable disagreement concerning what justice requires, it becomes very problematic to limit the moral right to civil disobedience to the promotion of what we consider to be morally good causes. The moral right to civil disobedience must therefore include a right to engage in civil disobedience in order to promote *wrongful* ends. An additional reason Lefkowitz gives is that, though we may wish to encourage agents to only autonomously choose morally good ends, the "only way to do so […] involves creating space within which agents may choose their ends, projects, and so on,"[36] be those ends good or bad. If we instead only grant agents the right to engage in political participation when we judge their decisions to be morally just, we are in effect denying them the possibility of an autonomous life.

I do not have the space here to discuss the merits of this argument with regard to civil disobedience, though there are certainly some problematic assumptions, particularly the strong claims that a state's authority is only legitimate if the state recognizes a moral right to civil disobedience,[37] and that treating its citizens as persons requires the state to acknowledge such a right.[38] Instead, what I wish to show is merely that this argument does not succeed in justifying a moral right to classified public whistleblowing.

4.2.4 *No moral right to classified public whistleblowing based on a moral right to do wrong*

As an, ideally, public-spirited breach of one's obligations, one might be inclined to view whistleblowing as a form of civil disobedience. Indeed, many scholars have taken this position.[39] In doing so, however, they overlook certain significant differences between whistleblowing and civil disobedience, which should lead us to reject any equation of the two. Most relevant for our purposes is, first, the observation that the *effects* are different: usually, an act of civil disobedience does not immediately result in the reform or repeal of the contested law. It is most often a long process that requires the involvement of a great many people, both within and without the sphere of government, to bring about change. By contrast, a whistleblower can, on their own, disclose a great many classified documents, thus immediately undoing the decision made by our democratically elected officials to have something kept secret. Second, civil disobedience and whistleblowing differ significantly concerning the possible *harm* they involve.[40] For example, the former does generally not involve a threat to national security, whereas this is a possibility in the case of classified public whistleblowing, given the nature of the documents disclosed. Additionally, unauthorized disclosures may result in harm to undercover agents or to ongoing military operations. These two important differences will lead me to conclude that, whatever the case may be regarding civil disobedience, there can be no moral right to whistleblowing based on a moral right to do wrong.

Let us start with fleshing out the implications of the first difference. The difference is that civil disobedience may, just as with whistleblowing, involve the violation of law, but that acts of civil disobedience do not immediately result in the repeal of the contested law. Whistleblowing, instead, immediately, performatively as it were, undoes the decision to classify certain information. What distinguishes whistleblowing from civil disobedience, then, is that it involves an *usurpation of power* – namely classification power – whereas civil disobedients merely protest a particular policy that they oppose and aim to have reformed or repealed entirely by the democratic authority. Whistleblowers can certainly have a similar aim, but the act of whistleblowing, in addition, involves the appropriation for themselves of the power to determine what ought and what ought not to be a legitimate state secret, whereas this is properly the prerogative of our democratically elected officials and not of private individuals. This renders whistleblowing wrongful in a way not imagined by Lefkowitz in his discussion of civil disobedience. The problem is not merely that whistleblowers may pursue morally problematic ends, but that, in whistleblowing, they arrogate to themselves political power that properly belongs to our democratic representatives. The question is whether the right to do wrong can also accommodate such wrongdoing.

The second difference between civil disobedience and whistleblowing was that the effects of whistleblowing may be more harmful than those of civil disobedience. Granting a moral right to whistleblowing that would include the right to disclose classified information even when it is the wrong thing to do (as is argued regarding the moral right to civil disobedience), is therefore not advisable. It is widely acknowledged among the advocates of a moral right to do wrong that certain wrongs are so grievous that they cannot be protected by the right.[41] It is my contention that the wrong involved in wrongful whistleblowing is precisely of this sort. An injudicious disclosure could have serious consequences, more so than an ill-advised exercise of civil disobedience. Naturally, there may be harm involved in civil disobedience, but the potential harm that could ensue from whistleblowing is of a different degree. Classified information may fall into the wrong hands, potentially endangering national security, field agents, or ongoing military operations. The case of Morton Seligman[42] offers a clear illustration of the risks involved in a right to engage in wrongful whistleblowing: during World War II, Seligman leaked decoded messages of the Imperial Japanese Navy to a journalist. Subsequently, the *Chicago Tribune* ran an article stating that the U.S. Navy was in the possession of details of the Japanese Navy's battle plans without, however, explicitly revealing the fact that the Americans had broken the Japanese code. Somehow, the Japanese never caught on, but if they had, Seligman's actions could have significantly harmed the American war effort, as the Japanese would almost certainly have developed another code. Given the possibility of such serious harm involved in wrongful disclosures, there can be no moral right to engage in wrongful or misguided whistleblowing, even with the help of a moral right to do wrong.

4.3 Conclusion

In this chapter I have argued that one of the most common defenses of whistleblowing,[43] which is based on individual rights, be they conceived as legal or moral rights, fails as a defense of whistleblowing. If the defense is based on *legal* rights it fails, first because there can be no such thing as a legal right to break the law; second, because the conception of rights involved in the defense deviates problematically from our common understanding of rights; and third, the legal rights-based defense misrepresents the reasons for offering some protection to whistleblowers: we do not wish to grant a defense on the basis that whistleblowing is a fundamental human interest to which all individuals have a right. Instead, we need to consider whether the unauthorized disclosures are of *public* importance; the defense ought to, therefore, not be based on individual rights but on the public role of whistleblowers.

Subsequently, granting the problematic position that moral rights need not necessarily be possible legal rights, and granting that it makes sense to speak of a moral right to do wrong (despite the availability of strong arguments against it), I have considered the argument for a moral right to civil disobedience, even when one's disobedience serves a cause that is less just than the status quo, in order to see whether it could be applied to the case of whistleblowing. I concluded that it could not, given two significant differences between civil disobedience and whistleblowing. First, it is doubtful that the right to do wrong can accommodate the usurpation of classification power in which whistleblowing consists and which sets it apart from civil disobedience. Second, due to the degree of wrongdoing involved in wrongful exercises of a supposed right to whistleblowing such a right is out of the question.

In closing, now that we have established that there are insurmountable problems with a defense of whistleblowing based on individual rights – be they moral or legal rights – we will need to find an alternative, more promising defense. This task will be undertaken in the next chapter.

Notes

1 This chapter draws from Boot, Eric R. 2018. No Right to Classified Public Whistleblowing. *Ratio Juris* 31: 70–85.
2 Voorstel van wet van de leden Van Raak, Fokke, Schouw, Segers, Ouwehand en Klein tot wijziging van de Wet Huis voor klokkenluiders (Proposal for an amendment of the Dutch Whistleblowing Protection Law). *Kamerstukken II* 2014/15, 34105, 7. p. 23.
3 Bowers QC, J., Fodder, M., Lewis, J., and Mitchell, J. 2007. *Whistleblowing: Law and Practice*. Oxford: Oxford University Press. 315; see section 1 (1) of the UK Official Secrets Act 1989.
4 5 USC § 2302(b)(8) (2012).
5 Indeed, to my knowledge no country grants citizens a right to legal protection from retaliation following a public unauthorized disclosure of classified materials.
6 See, e.g., Morse, M.C. 2010. Honor or Betrayal? The Ethics of Government Lawyer-Whistleblowers. *Georgetown Journal of Legal Ethics* 23: 421–54.
7 Open Society Foundations 2013. *The Global Principles on National Security and the Right to Information (Tshwane Principles)*. Retrieved from: https://www.opensocietyfoundations.org/publications/global-principles-national-security-and-freedom-information-tshwane-principles. Principle 1.
8 Different scholars and courts list different conditions. Some examples are: harm minimization, exhaustion of legal alternatives, the whistleblower's good faith, and, of course, that the disclosed information must contain evidence of wrongdoing of public concern.
9 See, e.g., Brownlee, K. 2012. *Conscience and Conviction: The Case for Civil Disobedience*. Oxford: Oxford University Press. 123. Though Brownlee does recognize a *moral* right to civil disobedience, which is equally puzzling, because, presumably, moral rights ought to be translatable into legal rights (however Brownlee rejects this presumption: ibid. 122ff.).
10 European Court of Human Rights (ECtHR) (Grand Chamber). *Guja v. Moldova*. February 12, 2008. Application no. 14277/04. § 76.
11 This shift in language from fundamental rights to public interests is of course already telling in itself: by, ultimately, appealing to public interests rather than rights, the drafters of the *Tshwane Principles*, inadvertently to be sure, demonstrate that a defense based on rights is not a sensible approach.
12 *Tshwane Principles*. Principle 43(a). A similar approach can be found in Kagiaros's proposal for a defense of whistleblowing: Kagiaros, D. 2015. Protecting "National Security" Whistleblowers in the Council of Europe: An

Evaluation of Three Approaches on How to Balance National Security with Freedom of Expression. *The International Journal of Human Rights* 19 (4): 408–28.

13 ECtHR. *Thorgeirson v. Iceland.* June 25, 1992. Application no. 13778/88. Para. 63.

14 Dworkin, R. 2011. *Justice for Hedgehogs.* Cambridge (Mass.): Belknap Press of Harvard University Press. 329.

15 See, e.g., Joseph Raz on the interest side of the rights debate – stating that rights occupy a special place in normative discourse due to their peremptory force (Raz, J. 1986. *The Morality of Freedom.* Oxford: Oxford University Press. 192) – as well as theorists such as H.L.A. Hart, for whom rights are about protecting a system of equal freedom, the great importance of which precludes any balancing of rights against public interests (Hart, H.L.A. 1955. Are There Any Natural Rights? *The Philosophical Review* 64 (2), 175–91. 191).

16 Benkler, Y. 2014. A Public Accountability Defense for National Security Leakers and Whistleblowers. *Harvard Law and Policy Review* 8, 281–326. 305. Santoro and Kumar refer to this same public role in order to argue for whistleblowers' legal right to protection (Santoro, Daniele, and Manohar Kumar. 2018. A Right to Protection for Whistle-Blowers. In *Claiming Citizenship Rights in Europe: Emerging Challenges and Political Agents.* Eds. Daniele Archibugi and Ali Emre Benli, 186–203. London: Routledge. 187). For the three reasons given above I find this problematic. It seems better to say instead that whistleblowing may be covered by a justification defense. In practice, this means that whistleblowing remains criminal. This enables the law to still attach significant risks to whistleblowing, which can help prevent the occurrence of frivolous and willfully false disclosures, while at the same time offering protection to those cases of whistleblowing that are justified. A justification defense, to be fully developed in Chapter 5, thus achieves the right balance between the prevention of undesirable acts and the protection of justified whistleblowing, allowing the latter to continue to fulfill its vital public function of bringing grave government wrongdoing to light. In short, there are both negative reasons to reject the proposal to grant whistleblowers legal rights to engage in whistleblowing and positive reasons in favor of the proposal to offer them instead a justification defense.

17 Raz, J. 1979. *The Authority of Law.* Oxford: Oxford University Press. 262: "if there is such a moral right then there is a presumption for giving it legal recognition."

18 Brownlee. *Conscience and Conviction.* 122–3. The right Brownlee has in mind is the right to civil disobedience.

19 Recall that according to the civic conception of civil servants' role obligations, an unauthorized disclosure does not constitute a violation of role obligations if said disclosure serves the public interest.

20 Waldron, J. 1981. A Right to Do Wrong. *Ethics* 92 (1), 21–39. 35.

21 Though perhaps one ought to speak of Hohfeldian "privileges," rather than rights. According to Hohfeld, if A has a privilege to Φ, then A is under no duty not to Φ. Furthermore, if A has a privilege to Φ, it follows that B has no right (or claim) that A refrain from Φ-ing. In short, Hohfeldian privileges (at times also referred to as "liberties") thus show what the holder of the privilege has no duty not to do (Hohfeld, W.N. (1913). Some Fundamental Legal Conceptions as Applied in Judicial Reasoning. *The Yale Law Journal* 23 (1): 16–59. 32ff.). So, for instance, I am under no duty to provide strangers with accurate directions to

the railway station. Conversely, they possess no right (i.e., no *claim*) to receive correct information from me.

22 Herstein, O.J. 2012. Defending the Right to Do Wrong. *Law and Philosophy* 31, 343–65. 355.

23 Waldron. *A Right to Do Wrong*. 36.

24 Kant, Immanuel. 1996. The Metaphysics of Morals. In *Practical Philosophy*. Ed. Mary Gregor, Trans. Mary Gregor, 353–603. Cambridge: Cambridge University Press. Ak 6: 226; cf. Kant, Immanuel. 1996. Groundwork of The Metaphysics of Morals. In *Practical Philosophy*. Ed. Mary Gregor, Trans. Mary Gregor, 37–108. Cambridge: Cambridge University Press. Ak 4: 447.

25 Raz. *The Morality of Freedom*. 381. Emphasis added.

26 Ibid. 411.

27 Galston, W.A. 1983. On the Alleged Right to Do Wrong: A Response to Waldron. *Ethics* 93 (2), 320–24. 322.

28 Raz. *The Authority of Law*. 268.

29 Lefkowitz, D. 2007. On a Moral Right to Civil Disobedience. *Ethics* 117 (2), 202–33. 224ff.; cf. Brownlee. *Conscience and Conviction*. 141.

30 Rawls, J. 2005. *Political Liberalism*. Expanded ed. New York: Columbia University Press. 58.

31 Lefkowitz. *Moral Right to Civil Disobedience*. 232.

32 Ibid. 213; cf. Lefkowitz, David. 2018. In Defense of Penalizing (but not Punishing) Civil Disobedience. *Res Publica* 24: 273–89.

33 Brownlee. *Conscience and Conviction*. 140ff.

34 Lefkowitz. *Moral Right to Civil Disobedience*. 213.

35 Ibid. 219.

36 Ibid. 227.

37 Ibid. 209.

38 Ibid. 219.

39 See, e.g., Brownlee, Kimberley. 2016. The Civil Disobedience of Edward Snowden: A Reply to William Scheuerman. *Philosophy and Social Criticism* 42: 965–70; cf. Scheuerman, William E. 2014. Whistleblowing as Civil Disobedience: The Case of Edward Snowden. *Philosophy and Social Criticism* 40: 609–28. Ten-Herng Lai, instead, maintains that whistleblowing is a form of *un*civil disobedience (Lai, Ten-Herng. 2019. Justifying Uncivil Disobedience. In *Oxford Studies in Political Philosophy. Volume 5*. Eds. David Sobel, Peter Vallentyne, and Steven Wall. Oxford: Oxford University Press. Forthcoming). By lumping it together with such forms of disobedience as ecotage and violent protest, however, it is clear that Lai overlooks the characteristic unique to whistleblowing, namely that it involves a usurpation of (classification) power, which properly belongs to our democratically elected officials (see the discussion of the first of the two differences between whistleblowing and civil disobedience below). Santoro and Kumar agree with me that whistleblowing cannot be reduced to a form of civil disobedience, but for different reasons: Santoro, Daniele, and Manohar Kumar. 2018. *Speaking Truth to Power – A Theory of Whistleblowing*. Switzerland: Springer International Publishing. 164ff.

40 Cf. Delmas, C. 2016, June 14. That Lonesome Whistle. *Boston Review*. Retrieved from: http://bostonreview.net/editors-picks-world-us/candice-delmas-lonesome-whistle.

41 See, e.g., Herstein. *Defending the Right to Do Wrong*. 359: "one's autonomy interests in a right to do wrong are most likely never weighty enough to justify a right to highly egregious wrongdoing."

42 Brennan, L.B. 2013. *Spilling the Secret – Captain Morton T. Seligman, US Navy (Retired), US Naval Academy Class of 1919*. Retrieved from: http://www.navy-history.org/2013/02/spilling-the-secret-captain-morton-seligman/.

43 Recall that when I speak of "whistleblowing" I intend "classified public whistleblowing."

5 Possible legal defenses for justified whistleblowing (2)

A public interest defense[1]

In the previous chapters we have seen that classified public whistleblowing is a *pro tanto* wrongful act that can, however, be morally justified if three conditions are met: the public interest condition, the *ultimum remedium* condition, and the minimization of harm condition. We have also seen that the most common legal defense of whistleblowing – namely a defense based on individual rights – is untenably problematic. However, given the vital social service provided by whistleblowers (namely providing the public with information revealing grave government wrongdoing), we would be well advised to provide whistleblowers with some measure of legal protection, lest a chilling effect causes future potential whistleblowers to refrain from disclosing government wrongdoing, leaving the public ignorant of abuses of power, human rights violations, and the like. Accordingly, this chapter will discuss another commonly proposed defense for whistleblowing: it is often said that unauthorized disclosures may be justified, and thus warrant legal protection against retaliation, if such disclosures reveal information that is *in the public interest*. In practice, this would involve setting up a criminal defense for whistleblowers. As a justification defense, such a "public interest defense" strikes a balance between, on the one hand, recognizing the importance of preventing undesirable disclosures of classified information (by maintaining the legal prohibition of whistleblowing) and, on the other hand, providing *justified* cases of whistleblowing the necessary legal protection so that we may continue to benefit in the future from disclosures that call the authority to account when it oversteps its bounds.

The main problem with this defense of justified whistleblowing is that the operative term – the public interest – is all too often left unclarified (by legal scholars, guidance documents, legislation, political philosophers). Chapter 3 has provided us with some much-needed clarity concerning the key concept of the public interest. It now remains for this chapter to ascertain the extent to which a legal justification defense of whistleblowing based on the public interest is feasible. Accordingly, the chapter will be structured as follows: Section 5.1 provides a description of how a public interest defense for whistleblowing could work, given the definition of the public interest expounded in Chapter 3. I argue that, for the legal defense to be fully available to the whistleblower, her disclosure must meet three conditions: the public interest condition, the *ultimum remedium* (or last resort) condition, and the minimize harm condition. If the first of these conditions is not met, the defense is unavailable. If, instead, only one of the latter two conditions is met (or if neither of them is met), the defense will likely serve to mitigate the sentence rather than function as a full defense. Section 5.2 discusses three possible objections to the public interest defense set out in Section 5.1: the epistemic constraints objection, the incommensurability of interests objection, and the reasonable disagreement objection. Section 5.3, finally, will further clarify the defense by applying it to a number of well-known cases of whistleblowing.

5.1 A public interest defense for whistleblowing

First of all, the public interest defense would be a justification defense. According to the most common understanding, when one claims one's action was *justified*, one concedes criminal wrongdoing, but denies that it was, all things considered, the wrong thing to do (e.g., *A* admits to having assaulted *B*, but argues that her action ought to be considered justified, given the fact that *B* had attacked her and she had acted out of self-defense). By comparison, when one invokes an *excuse*, one concedes that one's act was wrongful (both criminally and morally), but seeks to avoid the attribution of responsibility for the act (e.g., *A* admits to having wrongfully assaulted *B*, but *A*'s mental condition is such that it would be wrong to attribute responsibility for the act to *A*).[2] In practice, stating that unauthorized disclosures may be justified, means, according to this understanding of justification, that the act of whistleblowing remains criminal. This enables the law to still attach significant risks to whistleblowing, precluding (to an extent) the occurrence of frivolous and willfully false disclosures, while at the same time offering protection to those cases of whistleblowing that are justified. It, therefore, achieves the right balance between the prevention of undesirable acts and the protection of justified whistleblowing, allowing the latter to continue to fulfill its vital public function of bringing government wrongdoing to light.

In order to assess whether a particular whistleblower's disclosure of classified information to the media is justified, and thus ought not to incur any sanction, the judge must ask whether the release of the information did, on balance, more good than harm to the public interest as defined in Chapter 3, that is, the interest we share as members of the political community in those conditions that need to be in place if all members are to be able to pursue their own interests (e.g., the rule of law, the separation of powers, human rights). She must determine, in other words, whether disclosure or continued secrecy better serves those conditions. If the latter – if, in other words, the harm to the public interest caused by her disclosures likely outweighs the benefit to the public interest that would result from making the classified information public – then the whistleblower's actions are not covered by the defense. If the former, then her actions *are* covered by the defense, and criminal sanctions should either not be imposed at all or should be mitigated (depending on whether the further conditions of the defense, to be expounded in a moment, are met). Of course, this does not altogether do away with the problem of judicial discretion discussed in the introduction of Chapter 3, that is, the problem that applications of the public interest in whistleblowing cases are rather *ad hoc* and demonstrate "judicial idiosyncrasy." But it can *structure* that discretion by providing a framework for it. For example, the civic account of the public interest already excludes certain interests from consideration in the legal balancing test. Furthermore, it can help us determine which shared interests ought to be given a greater weight in the balancing test. One can imagine, if the public interest was simply determined as "interests shared by all," that it would be difficult to attach different weights to different public interests (as they all meet the key criterion of "being shared by all"). Instead, I have suggested that the public interest consists in the interest in the conditions that render it possible for each of us to develop and strive to realize our own values, objectives, and life plans. In realizing this possibility, some of these conditions are more important than others. Accordingly, we can attach varying weights to our sundry shared interests in accordance with how instrumental the conditions concerned are in facilitating the realization of our private interests. For example, good infrastructure is certainly in the public interest, for various reasons (because it makes trade possible, because it allows people to travel). Yet, if the only way to expand the current congested road network were to build a road through a natural reserve, which will seriously contaminate the most important clean water reservoir of the country, then such expansion is ultimately not in the public interest, given that clean water is a more fundamental condition for the possibility of pursuing our private interests (hereinafter: "a more fundamental condition" for short) than the ability to travel more quickly.

Of course, though excessive judicial discretion (where applications of the public interest become arbitrary, and potential whistleblowers consequently cannot with any certainty know in advance how the term "public interest" will be applied in their case) may thus be limited, some discretion will necessarily remain. It seems, for example, that different judges may reasonably disagree whether privacy is more in the public interest than security. Still, in the case of a real threat to national security, security will most likely be granted greater weight than privacy, showing that it is a more fundamental condition than privacy. After all, being alive and healthy is the *sine qua non* for the pursuit of our interests. However, determining where the public interest lies in a whistleblowing case will also require us to look at the *gravity* of the harm to security likely to ensue from disclosure and the *significance* of the benefit to privacy. If the former is quite small and the latter is rather large, then the public interest is ultimately best served by disclosure rather than continued secrecy. If, by contrast, the harm to national security is great and the benefit to privacy rather small, then the disclosure is not in the public interest. Finally, if the harm to national security and the benefit to privacy are judged to be more or less equal, then the public interest is best served by continued secrecy, given the greater weight attributed to national security.

In order to get a clearer idea of the proposed public interest defense, let us compare it with the "objective list approach," which is dominant in legal practice and scholarship.[3] This approach simply provides a list of values that may justify disclosures to the media of secret government actions, laws, or policies that threaten those values, if other avenues for addressing wrongdoing (internally, or externally to an independent oversight body) have been fruitlessly exhausted. Typically included on the list are, among others, human rights, political accountability, national security, and public health.[4] There are two problems with this approach. First, it does not do away with the problem it claims to solve. The (correct) point made by the objective list proponents is that we need to provide greater clarity for potential whistleblowers regarding the fundamental concept of the public interest. However, their approach fails to do this. After all, the various values on this list – human rights, public health, national security, etc. – may still conflict. The whistleblower will still have to judge for herself whether, for example, the benefits to privacy outweigh the harm to security brought about by her disclosure. In short, the uncertainty it set out to remove remains, because the objective list approach does not provide us any guidance in cases of conflict.[5] The whistleblower thus still has no way of determining which value ought to be granted more weight. My approach does provide such guidance, as it does not simply provide an *ad hoc* list of values possibly warranting disclosure; instead it gives a *reason* why those values are on the list, namely they are conditions that need to be in place if all members are to be able to pursue their own interests. This same reason also allows the whistleblower to attach different weights to different values and thus to determine which value is a "more fundamental condition" (as demonstrated in the two preceding paragraphs). Second, a limited list of specific values also risks being too rigid and thus insufficiently adaptable to new developments. Confronted with a new type of wrongdoing threatening a value not (yet) on the list, the objective list approach must deny protection to the whistleblower disclosing it. Again, my proposed account of the public interest does not suffer from this drawback, because it does not provide an ostensibly complete list of values justifying disclosure in the public interest, but instead a *theory* of the public interest that is equally applicable to new developments.

Still, even with the proposed account of the public interest, it might be difficult for, say, the average civil servant to ascertain whether the public interest would be better served by disclosure or continued secrecy. Of course, she could consult the relevant case law to get a sense of when the courts tend to grant protection to whistleblowers and when they do not. Yet, the case law may not be consistent[6] and the employee may also not be aware of the relevant rulings. In the latter case, the potential whistleblower may seek independent (legal) advice from a confidential adviser at one's workplace. As an alternative, the Netherlands has set up a so-called "House for whistleblowers" where potential whistleblowers can go for free and strictly confidential legal advice. Yet, even when such precautions are taken, mistakes can still be made: information may be disclosed, which the whistleblower *believed* would serve the public interest but which, in the end, does more harm than good to the public interest (or which, perhaps, does not point to government wrongdoing at all). Should a whistleblower in such a case still be allowed to invoke the public interest defense or should it only be available to those whose disclosures *actually* reveal wrongdoing and serve the public interest? Given the risks of a chilling effect, leading potential whistleblowers to err on the side of caution and thus to refrain from disclosing information even when it truly does reveal government wrongdoing, it would be best to allow the defense to be invoked in the former case as well, provided the information revealed could have *reasonably been believed* to reveal grave government wrongdoing. This concession need not lead to excessive whistleblowing, however, as the disclosure must pass both a *subjective* and an *objective* "reasonable belief" test. In other words, not only must the whistleblower herself have actually believed that her disclosure would be in the public interest,[7] but this subjectively held belief must, in addition, have been objectively reasonable. We must ask, therefore, whether a reasonable person[8] would have believed that the information demonstrated grave government wrongdoing that threatened one of the interests shared as members of the public, that is, threatened one of the key institutions that make it possible for each of us to develop life plans and strive to realize them. Furthermore, was it reasonable to believe that the benefit of informing the public of this wrongdoing would outweigh the possible detriment to those institutions or to particularly weighty private interests,[9] which could ensue from disclosing the information? If the answer is "no," then the objective reasonable belief test is not passed and the defense should therefore not be available to the whistleblower. This should filter out frivolous and deliberately false "disclosures." If, however, the whistleblower did all that could reasonably be expected of her to be sure that her disclosure would be in the public interest – i.e. assure herself that the information does indeed demonstrate grave government wrongdoing as well as engage conscientiously in the weighing exercise described above – if, in other words, her belief that her disclosure served the public interest was *reasonable*, then the defense ought still to be available.

Furthermore, I acknowledge that this approach may lead to some false positives (i.e., people disclosing information they shouldn't, yet still having the public interest defense available to them) and though this is of course problematic, I consider it less problematic than the alternative. If one punishes people who reasonably believed that they were blowing the whistle on grave government wrongdoing, the result will likely be overdeterrence: potential whistleblowers will prefer to err on the side of caution and thus to remain silent. Such a chilling effect risks depriving the public of crucial information concerning government wrongdoing.

A full public interest defense would contain two further conditions, already discussed in Chapter 3, constraining the *manner* in which a justified disclosure ought to be carried out. Though my main concern is with the public interest condition, I will briefly expound these two conditions here, for completeness' sake but also because they may help in allaying the concern (discussed in the previous paragraphs) that my approach would result in excessive whistleblowing. Before discussing these two *procedural conditions*, however, recall that the public interest condition must be understood as a *threshold condition*. That is to say, if it is not met, the defense immediately becomes unavailable. By contrast, the two *procedural conditions* determine whether the defense will function as a full defense or rather as a sentencing mitigation factor.

The *ultimum remedium condition* states that public disclosures ought to be a measure of last resort. One ought to first exhaust all alternative channels. In practice, this means one ought to first address the wrongdoing internally. In this manner, those in charge have the opportunity to investigate the wrongdoing and sanction those responsible or, alternatively, to explain why, in fact, no wrongdoing has occurred, without involving the public at large. This process can thus also help prevent public disclosures of information that either do not demonstrate wrongdoing, or that do demonstrate wrongdoing but where the potential benefits of the disclosures do not outweigh the potential costs. Such an internal investigation provides, after all, the first tests: is the information authentic? Does it demonstrate wrongdoing? Does disclosure of such wrongdoing outweigh the costs? In this manner, it can help prevent unauthorized disclosures that, upon reflection, are not in the public interest.

But, if one's complaint is not acted upon or if one reasonably believes the internal procedure to be infeasible (perhaps those responsible for the wrongdoing are able to influence or even block the internal investigation), one can then lodge one's complaints with an independent oversight body. This, too, makes it possible to address the wrongdoing in a confidential manner. If both alternative channels have been exhausted without result, or if the whistleblower reasonably believes that making the disclosure internally or to an independent oversight body will be in vain, or will lead to the destruction of evidence, or to reprisals against themselves or a third party, or if the information involved concerns an imminent risk or threat "to the life, health, and safety of persons, or to the environment,"[10] then the whistleblower may reveal the information to the public.

The *minimize harm condition* enjoins the whistleblower to take all possible steps to minimize the harm that may ensue from her disclosure. Especially when the information concerns matters of national security, unauthorized disclosures may cause substantial harm to undercover agents in the field, to ongoing military operations, and to national security. In order to mitigate such harm, the whistleblower would be wise to collaborate with established media outlets who can help edit the information so that only the information strictly necessary to reveal the wrongdoing is made public and nothing more. Experienced journalists can, furthermore, help determine the information's authenticity as well as present the information in such a manner so that the intended audience will adequately receive and comprehend it. The imposition of this condition is thus another way to prevent undesirable unauthorized disclosures. Together with the *ultimum remedium* condition and the objective "reasonable belief" test, it should go a long way in preventing unauthorized disclosures that are not in the public interest.

Note that I do not include a "good faith condition" in my proposed legal defense, though several whistleblower protection laws do contain such a condition.[11] The reason for the omission is simple and has already been given in Chapter 3: what matters is the *content* of the information. So long as the public interest condition has been fulfilled, it is irrelevant that the whistleblower's motives were not perfect. If disclosure serves the public interest, to be determined by the *objective* reasonable belief test, it does not matter that the whistleblower also had a private interest in disclosure. The thought is that a disclosure can still be in the public interest, even though it may *also* be in the private interest of the whistleblower. For example, Mark Felt's (a.k.a. Deep Throat's) disclosures, which would lead to the Watergate scandal, were still in the public interest, despite the fact that he was motivated (at least in part) by personal resentment (over having been passed over for promotion). The whistleblower need, therefore, not be a perfect Kantian agent who acts solely *aus Pflicht* (from duty) in order to benefit from the public interest defense. We need not require that her motivations were exclusively public-spirited. What we *should* require, however, is what has already been mentioned above, namely that the whistleblower must have actually held the belief that her disclosure would better serve the public interest than continued secrecy. The reason why is that such a *subjective* reasonable belief test renders the public interest defense unavailable to so-called "unknowing necessity cases."[12] *A*'s case constitutes a case of unknowing necessity if *A*'s disclosure is, as a matter of fact, necessary to avoid a greater threat to the public interest, but *A* acted in ignorance of this information. Imagine, for example, that *A* randomly discloses classified documents simply so *A* can impress *A*'s friends with *A*'s security clearance. As it happens, the information they disclose actually does more good than harm to the public interest. Still, we would not want the defense to be available to *A*. Our reasons could be both consequentialist (denying *A* the defense could help prevent *A*, and possibly others, through deterrence, from engaging in such frivolous disclosures in the future) and retributivist (by denying *A* the defense, we prevent *A* from getting away with such dangerous and irresponsible behavior). To sum up, the whistleblower need not have acted in good faith, understood as having perfect motivations. *A* must, however, have actually believed that *A*'s disclosure would be in the public interest.

Finally, if the whistleblower has met all three of the above conditions – public interest (consisting of both an objective and a subjective reasonable belief test), *ultimum remedium*, and minimize harm – to the best of her ability, then the only way the government can maintain its position that the unauthorized disclosure is unjustified (and the whistleblower, therefore, ought not to enjoy legal protection against retaliation) is by arguing that, for example, the whistleblower could not adequately assess where the public interest lies (with disclosure or with continued secrecy), because she did not have access to all the relevant information, causing her to overlook a specific and substantial harm to the public interest that outweighed any benefits to the public interest affected by the disclosure.

Before discussing possible objections to the public interest defense for classified public whistleblowing as provided in these pages, let us pause and take stock. The public interest defense is a justification defense. For the defense to be fully available to the whistleblower, her disclosure must meet three conditions: the public interest condition (consisting of both an objective and a subjective reasonable belief test), the *ultimum remedium* condition, and the minimize harm condition. If the first condition is not met, the defense is unavailable. If the latter two are not met, the defense will likely serve to mitigate the sentence rather than function as a full defense. For the public interest condition to be met, the benefit to the public interest brought about by the disclosure must outweigh the possible harm caused by it (or, at least, the whistleblower must have reasonably believed this to be the case). In practice, determining whether the public interest condition has been met, will often require weighing against each other competing interests we share as members of the public, which I have defined as interests in those conditions necessary for the possibility of pursuing our private interests. In cases of conflicting public interests (privacy and security, for example), the defense requires the judge to determine which of the competing shared interests involved is the more fundamental condition for the possibility of pursuing our private interests. Furthermore, it requires a determination of the *extent* of the harm done to security, say, or to particularly weighty private interests, and the *significance* of the benefit to privacy. Perhaps, generally speaking, we might say that security is a more fundamental condition than privacy, but if the detriment caused to the former by the disclosure is relatively small and the benefit to the latter is rather large, disclosure is still in the public interest and thus the defense ought to be available to the whistleblower. Finally, even if it turns that out no wrongdoing was involved, or that there was wrongdoing but the harm caused by the disclosure in fact outweighs the benefits brought about by it, the defense ought to still be available, provided that it was reasonable for the whistleblower to believe that her disclosure was in the public interest and that she actually held this belief.

5.2 Objections to the proposed defense

A first possible objection to this public interest defense for whistleblowing – let us call it the *epistemic constraints objection* – would argue that it demands too much of potential whistleblowers and judges: if a whistleblower wants her disclosures to be covered by the defense she will need to determine where the public interest lies and, in cases of conflict, which of the shared interests outweighs the other. Furthermore, she will need to make an assessment of the possible harm that could be precipitated by her disclosure and weigh that against the benefit to the public interest. Some might doubt that the average civil servant, for example, possesses all the relevant knowledge to make such an assessment. Lower-level civil servants in particular may not have access to all the information necessary to determine whether a secret policy involves grave harm to the public interest and whether disclosure would involve harm to national security, say, or to third parties. David Estlund would argue that in such circumstances the civil servant ought to refrain from disclosing the secret policy in question and respect its classified status, because it is the result of an institutional process with significant epistemic value. Our best evidence, he maintains, that a policy is morally acceptable is that it is the product of an institutional process designed to duly look after the question of whether it is just.[13] It follows that a civil servant acts wrongfully, for epistemic reasons, by substituting her own private judgment for the state's decision, which is the result of an institutional process with significant epistemic value. A public interest defense, according to this line of argument, would not be desirable as it would encourage civil servants to take it upon themselves to weigh the public interest in disclosure against the public interest in continued secrecy, whereas this is properly a *public* task, provided the political and institutional processes are aimed at arriving at the right answer.

There is some merit to this objection, and indeed I have already conceded that the determination of where the public interest lies is not without its difficulties. However, I have also pointed out that there are ways to attenuate this difficulty (e.g., by seeking out (legal) advice, and consulting the relevant case law). Furthermore, there are plenty of cases of relatively straightforward wrongdoing: Watergate, Abu Ghraib, political corruption. In these and similar cases, the fact that the individual civil servant does not possess all the facts is not likely to be an obstacle to adequate moral judgment.

A further reply to this objection is that often a civil servant may feel compelled to blow the whistle *precisely because* the institutional procedures that are usually abided by, and which, according to Estlund, produce authoritative commands due to their "effort and tendency to get the right answer,"[14] are set aside or are defective. As an example, consider the executive's decision to wage war without first consulting and obtaining approval from the legislature. In such a case, Estlund's argument would no longer apply as the very procedure that results in authoritative commands has been bypassed.[15]

The second objection concerns what Rahul Sagar has termed the "*incommensurability of interests.*"[16] He argues that there is no firm basis on which we can weigh, for example, the public interest in security (which presumably calls for secrecy, at times) against the public interest in political accountability (which requires transparency). This, too, is a valid point. It is my hope, however, that the civic account of the public interest (defense) expounded in this chapter and Chapter 3 can be a guide in what Sagar describes as the "messy reality" of interest balancing.[17] It allows us, first of all, to identify public interests as interests that we share as members of the public in the conditions that render it possible for each of us to develop and strive to realize our own values, objectives, and life plans. Furthermore, it enables us to attach different weights to our various shared interests in accordance with how instrumental the conditions concerned are in facilitating the realization of our private interests. The more fundamental a condition is for the possibility of pursuing our private interests, the greater the weight that ought to be attached to it. In deciding, finally, whether disclosure or continued secrecy best serves the public interest, we ought also to consider the degree of harm involved with disclosure and the magnitude of the benefit.

Now, Sagar is of course right to point out that all this may present difficulties for a judge who has to decide whether a particular unauthorized disclosure was in the public interest. But I am more optimistic regarding the courts' ability to reach such a decision. They are generally quite able to deal with complex and controversial issues. In hate speech cases, for example, the judge must also undertake a complicated balancing test: she will need to weigh the value of the individual's right to freedom of expression against the harm that individual's hateful speech is believed to cause to an already marginalized ethnic or religious minority. The harm involved is often not very concrete or specific. Yet, the court will have to attach a particular weight to it and consider whether the prevention of such harm outweighs the value of free speech. Similarly, Heidi Kitrosser wonders whether whistleblowing cases are really more complex than the intricate environmental, scientific, and financial cases, which courts are deemed capable of dealing with.[18]

Despite the courts' general ability to successfully deal with complex cases, however, their application of the public interest in whistleblowing cases thus far has been criticized as *ad hoc* and idiosyncratic. Yet, the problem was not so much the courts' judgments or their ability to study complex documents, but rather that they had to exercise their otherwise considerable capabilities in the dark, as it were, with few to no guidelines to assist them. It is precisely this lack that the civic account of the public interest (defense) aims to remedy. The guidance provided by it, combined with the courts' substantial abilities, should be sufficient to adequately deal with public interest defenses of whistleblowing, or at the very least to improve the courts' disappointing track record so far. The complexity of weighing interests against each other, therefore, does not warrant the abandonment of the public interest defense as expounded here.

The third objection – the *reasonable disagreement objection* – does not so much argue that the judge or the whistleblower is in no position to determine where the public interest lies due to epistemic constraints (as with the first objection), but rather that, even if she were in possession of all the relevant facts, there could still very well be reasonable disagreement concerning the conclusions that ought to be drawn from those relevant facts. Informed people may still disagree over whether a given classified policy constitutes a threat to the public interest and thus whether its disclosure serves the public interest or not. Providing a defense, the key term of which, so this argument goes, is necessarily open to interpretation, will only generate more disputes than it settles. Furthermore, the ambiguity of the central concept will make it all the easier for a government to dismiss a whistleblower's appeal to the public interest as "just another interpretation." In short, a public interest defense will not resolve anything, due to the indeterminate nature, so the argument goes, of the public interest.

Once again, my first reply would be that there are plenty of cases of uncontroversial wrongful government conduct (e.g., abuse of power, political corruption, Abu Ghraib, Watergate). Such cases are not susceptible to this counterargument.

Furthermore, reasonable disagreement does not necessarily present an argument against disclosure if the wrongdoing in question is *procedural* rather than (exclusively) substantial. For example, the problem with the government's implementation of a secret large-scale domestic surveillance program is not only that some might deem it unjust, but rather that such a policy is a matter of public concern (as it impacts fundamental rights), about which, accordingly, the public ought to be informed. If what matters is that citizens are able to form an opinion concerning the policy in question through public debate,[19] which is made impossible by the policy's secret nature, then reasonable disagreement concerning the policy's desirability is not an argument against disclosure.

Finally, though there can be no disagreement over which interests are *public* interests (according to the civic account defended here, public interests are interests in those conditions that render it possible for each of us to develop and strive to realize our own values, objectives, and life plans), it is possible for there to be disagreement over the weight we ought to attach to our various shared interests. But is this a problem for the functioning of the defense? I believe it is not. Recall that the whistleblower who wishes to benefit from the defense need not show that her assessment of what better serves the public interest – disclosure or continued secrecy – is ultimately the correct one. Instead, she needs to demonstrate that she had a reasonable belief that her disclosure revealed a threat to the public interest and that the benefits of disclosure would outweigh the possible associated harms to the public interest. (Recall, too, that our reason for this approach was to avoid a chilling effect.) It follows that *reasonable* disagreement (between the whistleblower and the government) over the weight to be assigned to competing public interests cannot be grounds for denying the whistleblower the defense. Indeed, typically this is not the approach taken by governments. Often they will decide to prosecute a whistleblower *not* because the whistleblower incorrectly attached more weight to privacy than to security, for example, but rather because her disclosures allegedly damaged national security more than she had (or even could have) foreseen. In other words, the problem is not so much that the whistleblower attached too little weight to the shared interest of security, say, but rather that she made an incorrect assessment of the harm that might ensue from her disclosure. The whistleblower may thus fail to meet the second procedural condition (after all, *minimizing harm* presupposes a sincere effort to adequately assess the possible harm). In this case, the defense could at most function only as a sentence mitigating factor. However, the whistleblower might also fail to meet the first condition (the *public interest condition*). This condition requires weighing the benefits of disclosure against its possible harmful consequences. If the whistle-blower was negligent in making the assessment of the potential harm that might be caused by her disclosure, then she was in no position to execute this weighing exercise in a satisfactory manner. Accordingly, she does not meet the public interest condition either, and so does not have the defense available to her at all. But the burden of proof here lies on the government to demonstrate that the unauthorized disclosure has indeed caused far more harm to the public interest than foreseen by the whistleblower, and that this harm outweighs the benefits of disclosure.

In sum, typically, the argument the government would make is not that we ought to attach a greater weight to security than to privacy or political accountability, say, but rather that the whistleblower has made an incorrect assessment (perhaps negligently so) of the harm that might ensue from her disclosure. It is thus not primarily a matter of reasonable disagreement over values, but rather of incorrect assessment of harm. The reasonable disagreement objection, therefore, misses the mark.

5.3 Application to case studies

Having elaborately expounded and argued for the three justifying conditions of the public interest defense, I will, in closing, apply this defense to three case studies in order to demonstrate how it would function in practice. Recall that Chapter 3 proposed a distinction between the threshold condition (i.e., the public interest condition) and the two procedural conditions. Recall further that this chapter has suggested that, depending on whether all conditions are met or only the threshold condition, the public interest defense can function either as a full defense or as a sentence mitigating factor, respectively. This allows us to view eligibility for the defense as a matter of degree.

5.3.1 Samuel L. Morison – no defense

In 1985 Samuel L. Morison, a naval intelligence analyst, provided *Jane's Defense Weekly* with classified satellite pictures of a Soviet aircraft carrier.[20] This case is relatively straightforward: given that the information he disclosed did not reveal (nor could reasonably have been considered to reveal) government wrongdoing and so did not serve the public interest, the threshold condition is not met. The defense is therefore not available.

5.3.2 Chelsea Manning – sentence mitigation

In 2010, Chelsea (formerly Bradley) Manning dumped 750,000 documents online by leaking them to WikiLeaks. These included diplomatic cables, incident reports from Afghanistan and Iraq, and a video showing a U.S. Army helicopter repeatedly opening fire on a group of people, thereby killing two Reuters journalists and twelve civilians. Manning had not redacted the names of people mentioned in the incident reports from Iraq, and the documents in general were placed online without sufficient editing. According to U.S. officials, this endangered the lives of those who supported the U.S. military. They, furthermore, argued that if diplomacy is to function properly, people need to be able to speak in confidence. Ensuring such confidentiality has become problematic because of these disclosures (widely known as Cablegate). Additionally, Cablegate has supposedly made certain countries reluctant to exchange intelligence with the United States.

We should by no means accept the official response unquestioningly, but we can nevertheless assert that Manning (and WikiLeaks) did not do enough to meet the minimize harm condition. The State Department cables, for example, "'outed' many individuals who put themselves at considerable risk by confiding in embassy officials in countries with repressive regimes or internal strife."[21] Furthermore, Manning and WikiLeaks did not limit the disclosures to the information strictly necessary to demonstrate government wrongdoing. Instead, the majority of the leaks did not contain information that was of public concern.[22] The leaked diplomatic cables, in particular, included a lot of embassy gossip.[23] Moreover, instead of disclosing the information with the help of established media outlets who could have edited the information and provided the necessary context, Manning passed the documents to WikiLeaks who placed them online in their entirety.

It is unclear whether there was a viable internal option for addressing the wrongdoing that concerned Manning. Under the Military Whistleblower Protection Act, however, Manning could have made her disclosures to a member of Congress or an Inspector General, for example, but she did not take this route. In fact, in court she admitted that she "had a lot of alternatives,"[24] which she did not pursue. The *ultimum remedium* condition has, therefore, also not been met.

Manning's disclosures, however, certainly *did* contain information that disclosed grave government wrongdoing. The incident reports, for instance, suggested that there were far more civilian casualties in Afghanistan and Iraq than the United States had admitted to, that there were "dozens of instances of admitted 'excessive force' during the [Iraq] occupation,"[25] and that the American military was directly implicated in Iraqi detainee abuse and torture.[26] So the question facing us is what, in this case, would better serve the public interest: disclosure or continued secrecy? Keeping the information above out of the public eye rendered it impossible for the American people to hold those responsible for such excesses to account. This is particularly problematic, given that these excesses of force and violations of human rights were supposedly carried out in the name of the American people. Disclosure thus certainly promoted the shared interest of public accountability. These excesses of force and human rights violations, furthermore, could also be viewed as constituting a threat to the national security of the United States, given that they tend to cause anti-American sentiments in the countries where they occur, which some might express in violent ways. Allowing these actions to continue unchecked and largely in secret (from the American perspective, at least), therefore, without any way of bringing them to an end (given the absence of public accountability), could thus harm the shared interest of national security. Moreover, continued secrecy endangers the interest Americans share in governing themselves. When the American government hides its involvement in, to put it euphemistically, morally highly questionable practices, such as human rights violations, from the American people and their representatives, it fails to treat its subjects as equals, because it does not accord the democratic rights of citizens sufficient respect. Practices of such great magnitude and for which the moral nature is so extremely problematic, ought to be publicly debated, as far as possible and at the very least behind closed doors, by the representatives of the public in Congress. Manning's disclosures of *these* documents thus not only benefited the shared interests of public accountability and national security, but also that of democratic self-governance. As such, they were in the public interest. Consequently, Manning appears to be eligible for the public interest defense.

But did Manning's disclosure not harm the public interest as well, particularly the shared interest in national security? Initially, this is what the U.S. government argued, but, in the end, the Department of Defense concluded that Manning's disclosures had not revealed any sensitive intelligence sources or methods. There was, furthermore, no indication that any of the Afghans named in the disclosed documents were retaliated against by the Taliban.[27] Nonetheless, Manning failed to take sufficient steps to minimize harm, which could have had more serious consequences. That, and the fact that the greater part of the leaked documents did not reveal gross wrongdoing and that Manning did not pursue alternatives to unauthorized disclosure, render the public interest defense unavailable to her as a complete defense, as the two procedural conditions have not been met. It could, however, serve to *mitigate* her sentence. Given the greater weight accorded to the threshold condition on my account, which (part of) her disclosures meet, Manning's 35 years' prison sentence was far too severe (and it has indeed since been commuted by former President Barack Obama, leading to her release on May 17, 2017, seven years after she was arrested on a base outside Baghdad).

5.3.3 Edward Snowden – complete defense

Instead of simply placing unedited documents online, Snowden enlisted the help of several journalists (most notably, *The Guardian*'s Glenn Greenwald and Ewen MacAskill), ProPublica, and filmmaker Laura Poitras, to reveal the NSA's mass surveillance programs. The media involved edited the material thoroughly before publishing and provided the necessary context to the great flood of information. Snowden thus certainly took steps to minimize the harm that could result from his disclosures.

Snowden has stated, furthermore, that he voiced his concerns regarding certain surveillance programs to his superiors on several occasions, but that nothing was done with his complaints and he was told it was not his job to make such ethical judgments.[28] There are further alternatives to public disclosures, but intelligence community employees in general have relatively few protections against retaliation, and this is especially true of intelligence community *contractors*, such as Snowden.[29] Furthermore, raising concerns either internally in the NSA, or externally by approaching members of the congressional intelligence committees, would most likely also have been fruitless as both officials within the NSA and members of the intelligence committees were already aware of the NSA activities that worried Snowden. Indeed, the NSA Inspector General, who is authorized to receive and investigate complaints from potential whistleblowers, has publicly stated that if Snowden had voiced his concerns with him, he would simply have told Snowden that the NSA was acting within the bounds of the law.[30] The *ultimum remedium* condition is, therefore, not an obstacle to successfully mounting the public interest defense in Snowden's case.

It goes without saying that government surveillance, whereby citizens' telephone and internet records were monitored on a massive scale, is a matter of public concern. Fundamental rights, such as the right to privacy, were curtailed by these government policies, putting at risk the interest we share as members of the public in having a sphere of protected free agency, which is ensured by fundamental rights. By disclosing these government policies to the larger public, Snowden sparked a debate concerning the proper bounds of government surveillance on the one hand and the scope of fundamental rights on the other. Furthermore, two different judges, as mentioned in Chapter 1, have deemed the NSA's data collection program unconstitutional and illegal, Congress has felt compelled to pass the USA Freedom Act, which introduced vital reforms to the NSA's bulk data collection program, and the UN General Assembly declared online privacy to be a fundamental human right. All this demonstrates that Snowden's disclosures did indeed reveal grave government wrongdoing to the public and that they in fact benefited the shared interest we have in our fundamental rights. By informing the public of secret government policies that impact fundamental rights, Snowden's disclosures additionally benefited the shared interest in public accountability.

On the other hand, we need to consider whether Snowden's actions harmed a different shared interest, namely that of national security. The President's Review Group on Intelligence and Communications Technologies has maintained that some of the bulk data collection programs disclosed by Snowden did actually play a role in preventing terrorism. For example, Section 702 of the Foreign Intelligence Surveillance Act (allowing the targeting of the communications of non-U.S. persons residing outside of the United States for foreign intelligence purposes, though indirectly it may also target the international communications of U.S. citizens) has helped gather intelligence which led to over 50 counterterrorism investigations. The President's Review Group is convinced that Section 702 did in fact "play an important role in the nation's effort to prevent terrorist attacks across the globe,"[31] and is worried that the exposure of this program may have inhibited its functioning. Given that Section 702 was reauthorized in January 2018, however, it seems that Snowden's disclosures have not greatly affected its efficacy, at least not in the long term. Indeed, the harm of disclosure is likely to be limited to the "adaptation of techniques to recover lost effectiveness."[32] It seems unlikely that such a cost would outweigh the infringement of the fundamental rights of millions of people, both at home and abroad. Furthermore, it remains an open question whether the success that (some of) the NSA's surveillance programs may have had, is achieved "in a way that unnecessarily sacrifices individual privacy and damages foreign relations."[33] Public discussion of that question is precisely what Snowden aimed to spark with his revelations, thus also benefiting the public interest in democratic self-governance, which requires public discussion of matters of public concern.

All told, Snowden's disclosures appear to have benefited the public interest more than the alternative – continued secrecy – would have. The threshold condition has thus been met, as have the two procedural conditions, rendering Snowden's disclosures an eligible candidate for a complete defense under the public interest defense, as developed here.

5.4 Conclusion

This chapter set out to determine whether a public interest defense is feasible and desirable. Section 5.1 provided a description of the public interest defense.

Section 5.2 showed that this defense is not without its difficulties. However, I also hope that my replies to these objections discussed in the same section, as well as my application of the public interest defense to three case studies in Section 5.3, have demonstrated that such a defense is certainly workable and feasible. The civic account of the public interest provides sufficient guidance for judges to undertake the necessary balancing test. This ought to do away with the excesses of judicial discretion, which at present leads to legal uncertainty, and which, in turn, may lead potential whistleblowers to refrain from disclosing government wrongdoing for fear of retaliation. The defense is, therefore, indispensable (and thus desirable). Without it, we risk depriving ourselves of what has become the most important source for finding out about government wrongdoing. In sum, the public interest defense, despite its difficulties (which I have shown to be generally surmountable), is feasible as well as necessary. Moreover, it is our only option to provide protection to justified cases of classified public whistleblowing, given the untenability of a rights-based defense (as demonstrated in Chapter 4).

Notes

1 This chapter draws from Boot, Eric R. 2019. The Feasibility of a Public Interest Defense for Whistleblowing. *Law and Philosophy.* Forthcoming. It also draws from Boot, Eric R. 2017. Classified Public Whistleblowing: How to Justify a *pro tanto* Wrong. *Social Theory and Practice* 43: 541–67.

2 For such an account of the distinction between justifications and excuses, see, e.g.: Austin, J.L. 1956. A Plea for Excuses: The Presidential Address. *Proceedings of the Aristotelian Society* 57: 1–30. 2; Fletcher, George P. 2000. *Rethinking Criminal Law.* Oxford: Oxford University Press. 759.

3 Note that I am not referring here to objective list theories of *well-being* as discussed by philosophers, particularly utilitarians. Instead, I am simply referring to the common approach found in whistleblower protection legislation and guidance documents to draw up lists of values that may warrant disclosure.

4 See, for example, Benkler, Yochai. 2014. A Public Accountability Defense for National Security Leakers and Whistleblowers. *Harvard Law and Policy Review* 8: 281–326. 308–9; Kagiaros, Dimitrios. 2015. Protecting "National Security" Whistleblowers in the Council of Europe: An Evaluation of Three Approaches on How to Balance National Security with Freedom of Expression. *The International Journal of Human Rights* 19: 408–28. 420; Open Society Foundations. 2013. *The Global Principles on National Security and the Right to Information (Tshwane Principles).* Available at: https://www.opensociety-foundations.org/publications/global-principles-national-security-and-freedom-information-tshwane-principles. Principle 10; UK Information Commissioner's Office. 2016. *The Public Interest Test: Freedom of Information Act.* 6.

5 Indeed, some of its proponents admit as much: Kagiaros. Protecting "National Security" Whistleblowers. 421.

6 David Lewis has shown the case law concerning the public interest in whistle-blowing cases to be inconsistent (Lewis, David. 2015. Is a Public Interest Test

for Workplace Whistleblowing in Society's Interest? *International Journal of Law and Management* 57: 141–58).

7 I will explain why I include this subjective test below.

8 The description of the "reasonable belief" test here relies on Arthur Ripstein's account of the "reasonable person" as the person "who exercises *appropriate foresight* in deciding whether to engage in activities that impose risks on others." To do so involves taking both the benefits (in this case, to the public interest) and the likely costs into account (Ripstein, Arthur. 1994. Equality, Luck, and Responsibility. *Philosophy & Public Affairs* 23: 3–23. 11–12).

9 Think, for example, of a disclosure that would also reveal the identity of under-cover intelligence officers, exposing them to grave harm.

10 *Tshwane Principles*. 2013. Principle 40a.

11 See, e.g., the case law of the European Court of Human Rights. For example ECtHR, *Guja v. Moldova*, § 77; ECtHR, *Heinisch v. Germany*, no. 28274/08, §§ 82–7, 2011; ECtHR, *Bucur and Toma v. Romania*, no. 40238/02, §§ 116–18, 2013).

12 For interesting discussions of such cases see, e.g.: Alexander, Larry. 2005. Lesser Evils: A Closer Look at the Paradigmatic Justification. *Law and Philosophy* 24: 611–643; Berman, Mitchell N. 2005. Lesser Evils and Justification: A Less Close Look. *Law and Philosophy* 24: 681–709.

13 Estlund, David. 2007. On Following Orders in an Unjust War. *The Journal of Political Philosophy* 15: 213–34. 222.

14 Ibid. 221.

15 Indeed, Estlund seems to concede this point and even argues that "[s]oldiers lower down in the chain of command also have a responsibility to ask themselves whether justice is being looked after" (ibid. 226), that is, whether the institutional and procedural safeguards are functioning properly.

16 Sagar, Rahul. 2013. *Secrets and Leaks: The Dilemma of State Secrecy*. Princeton: Princeton University Press. 120.

17 Ibid.

18 Kitrosser, Heidi. 2008. Classified Information Leaks and Free Speech. *University of Illinois Law Review* 3: 881–932. 913: "In such [complex] cases, parties bring the courts up to speed through evidence and briefings. Among the judiciary's strengths in this respect are its familiarity with studying complex factual records and accompanying briefings, its ability to demand additional information and expert assistance from the parties, and its ability to call in court-appointed experts for additional assistance."

19 Of course, the government need not (and at times ought not to) publicize each and every detail concerning the secret policy, as that might very well undermine the policy's functioning, endanger national security, or have other undesirable effects. Often, however, the government can disclose the general contours of the policy, which can safely be the subject of public debate. Dennis Thompson refers to this as "partial secrecy" (Thompson, Dennis F. 1999. Democratic Secrecy. *Political Science Quarterly* 114: 181–93).

20 Toner, Robin. 1985. Naval Analyst Is Guilty of Espionage. *The New York Times*, October 18. Retrieved from: https://www.nytimes.com/1985/10/18/us/naval-analyst-is-guilty-of-espionage.html.

21 Cole, David. 2014. The Three Leakers and What to Do About Them. *The New York Review of Books*, February.

22 Benkler. *Public Accountability Defense*. 320.

23 For example, the American diplomats' assessment of Silvio Berlusconi as "feckless, vain and ineffective as a modern European leader" is not of public concern (Busch, Michael. 2015. Europe. In *The WikiLeaks Files: The World According to US Empire 2*, 181–211. London: Verso. 181).
24 Bouchard, Chad. 2013. Manning Pleads Guilty, Saying He Hoped to Spark Public Debate. *100Reporters*, March 1. Retrieved from: https://100r.org/2013/03/manning-pleads-guilty-saying-he-hoped-to-spark-public-debate/
25 Jamail, Dahr. 2015. Iraq. In *The WikiLeaks Files: The World According to US Empire*, 350–67. London: Verso. 352.
26 Ibid. 363.
27 This assessment of the consequences of Manning's leaks was presented by then-Secretary of State Robert Gates to the Chairman of the Senate Armed Services Committee; it was based on a thorough Pentagon review of the documents Manning disclosed: Levine, Adam. 2010. Gates: Leaked Documents Don't Reveal Key Intel, but Risks Remain. *CNN*, October 17. Retrieved from: http://www.cnn.com/2010/US/10/16/wikileaks.assessment/index.html.
28 Greenwald, Glenn. 2015. *No Place to Hide: Edward Snowden, the NSA and the Surveillance State*. London: Penguin Books. 42.
29 PEN American Center. 2015. *Secret Sources: Whistleblowers, National Security, and Free Expression*. 9. Retrieved from: https://pen.org/sites/default/files/Secret%20Sources%20report.pdf
30 Ibid. 10.
31 The President's Review Group on Intelligence and Communications Technologies. 2013. *Liberty and Security in a Changing World*. December 12. 145. Retrieved from: https://obamawhitehouse.archives.gov/sites/default/files/docs/2013-12-12_rg_final_report.pdf
32 Benkler. *Public Accountability*. 322.
33 President's Review Group. *Liberty and Security*. 145.

6 Obligatory whistleblowing[1]

> *For, however virtuous someone is, all the good that he can ever perform still is merely duty; to do one's duty, however, is no more than to do what lies in the common moral order and is not, therefore, deserving of wonder. This admiration is, on the contrary, a dulling of our feeling for duty, as if to give obedience to it were something extraordinary and meritorious.*[2]

Thus far, we have clarified why whistleblowing is a *pro tanto* morally wrongful act, under what conditions it may nonetheless be justified, and what legal defense for justified cases of whistleblowing is most promising. In all of this, it seems we have presupposed that whistleblowing can, at best, be *permissible*. But can it also be a matter of *obligation*? Can one be blamed, in other words, for *not* blowing the whistle? This is the main question the present chapter sets out to answer. More specifically, it wishes to inquire whether civil servants, the main agents of classified public whistleblowing, who are complicit in government wrongdoing, incur a *moral obligation* to remedy the injustice they have contributed to by disclosing it. Note that I am here interested in *moral* (not legal) obligations, and that I wish to establish whether civil servants complicit in government wrongdoing incur a moral *obligation* (rather than a *duty*) to disclose. In using the word "obligation" instead of "duty" here, I follow the familiar distinction between the two, known from the works of Hart and Rawls, among others: obligations are voluntarily incurred, that is, as a consequence of our own actions, whereas duties are held prior to and irrespective of the agent's behavior.[3] In other words, I am only interested in the obligation to blow the whistle, which we incur as a consequence of our own wrongful conduct, *not* in a freestanding duty to blow the whistle because it may simply be the right thing to do. The strategic reason for this is that often whistleblowing is viewed as a supererogatory or even heroic act, due to the risks involved to the whistleblower herself. I wish to confute this view by demonstrating that, at the very least, we may have an *obligation* to blow the whistle on government wrongdoing if we are complicit in that wrongdoing.

As said, when whistleblowing is discussed in the philosophical literature, the main question is nearly always "Is it permissible?" (and the same can be said for civil disobedience,). The important question whether one can ever have an *obligation* to engage in whistleblowing or civil disobedience is thus ignored. Regarding civil disobedience, there are a few rare exceptions.[4] These works, however, do not discuss our obligations to engage in civil disobedience in the context of our responsibility for collective wrongdoing, but instead base the obligation to civil disobedience on an expanded notion of political obligation. As I am concerned in this chapter with the obligation of civil servants to disclose secret government wrongdoing in which they are complicit, these texts are, therefore, of little help.

Political philosophical discussions of classified public whistleblowing in general are in short supply, but when political philosophers do discuss it, they, again, limit themselves to the question whether it is ever permissible.[5] I know of but one example that deals with the question of a *duty* to blow the whistle,[6] but here, again, the duty is not founded on the complicity of civil servants in collective wrongdoing. Others have focused on a duty to address wrongdoing either internally or externally through a supervisory body.[7] What I am interested in, however, is not whether there can be a duty to engage in entirely legal methods of addressing wrongdoing. Indeed, many countries already have imposed a legal obligation upon civil servants to disclose "waste, fraud, abuse, and corruption to appropriate authorities."[8] Instead, I wish to take on the thornier question of whether there can ever be an obligation to disclose state secrets to the public (typically, via the media).

In business ethics, it is a bit more common to consider *obligations* to disclose wrongdoing, but accounts that base such an obligation on one's complicity in collective wrongdoing, are rare. Michael Davis is one who *does* argue for an obligation to disclose wrongdoing if one is complicit in it,[9] yet he offers no substantial account of responsibility for collective wrongdoing in which one is complicit that would help us establish if a given person has an obligation to disclose wrongdoing and, if so, how strong that obligation would be.

This chapter thus wishes to fill a lamentable lacuna; it wishes to establish, specifically, whether civil servants who are complicit in government wrongdoing incur a moral obligation to remedy the injustice they have contributed to by disclosing it, and, if they do, what the nature and strength of this obligation are. My contention will be that they do have such an obligation, but that it is defeasible, and that its strength (and thus the likelihood of its being defeated) depends on the blameworthiness of one's complicity.

Accordingly, the argument will proceed as follows: first, I will argue that one is responsible for collective wrongdoing insofar as one is complicit in it. Second, I will demonstrate that civil servants can indeed be held responsible for government wrongdoing in which they are complicit, by way of the consideration and refutation of three counterarguments. Third, I will briefly establish that responsibility for wrongdoing (including collective wrongdoing) gives rise to obligations of remedy. Fourth, I will consider six possible strategies to fulfill one's obligation of remedy as a civil servant who has contributed to government wrongdoing, concluding that unauthorized disclosures generally appear to be the most effective, given that I am concerned with *secret* government wrongdoing. I acknowledge, however, that other strategies may, at times, be more effective. Accordingly, the fifth section establishes, by way of the refutation of several counterarguments, that *when disclosure is the most effective way of addressing the wrongdoing*, civil servants who are complicit in classified government wrongdoing do indeed incur an obligation to disclose such wrongdoing. This obligation will turn out to be a *pro tanto* obligation, liable to be defeated by countervailing moral reasons. In the sixth step of the argument, I will discuss two examples in order to demonstrate how we can assess the strength of the obligation to disclose. The general idea is that the more blameworthy one's complicity is, the stronger one's *pro tanto* obligation of remedy will be, and the more difficult it will be for this obligation to be outweighed by other moral considerations. Hereby, I largely follow Lepora and Goodin (see below) in viewing the blameworthiness of one's complicity as a function of (1) the badness of the principal wrongdoing, (2) the responsibility for the contributory act, and (3) the extent of the contribution. I will end by considering the case of bystanders to government wrongdoing, arguing that omissions can also be causally effective, and thus that bystanders' culpable silence may amount to complicity in wrongdoing as well.

1. *One is responsible for collective wrongdoing, to the extent that one is complicit in it*

It has often been pointed out – for example in the sprawling literature concerning the duties of well-off individuals toward the global poor – that our moral intuitions seem most suitable to a type of social organization characterized mainly by small-scale and direct interactions that are by no means exhaustive of all our dealings in a globalized world. Accordingly, we tend to view acts as enjoying primacy over omissions, near effects over remote effects, and individual effects over group effects.[10] This chapter will only be concerned with the last of these relations (and very briefly with the first, at the very end of the chapter): one tends to view those outcomes for which one is solely responsible as implicating oneself to a far larger degree than those with regard to which one's actions amounted to but one of the many contributing factors alongside the actions of a number of other agents. On the classic view of responsibility for harm, my own actions ought to be the sufficient condition for the harm in question.[11] This view poses clear problems for individual responsibility for *collective* wrongdoing, i.e. wrongdoing for which, by definition, no one agent is exhaustively responsible. This is not "merely" a theoretical shortcoming: a significant part of contemporary wrongdoing is the product of collective action, often mediated by institutions. But if we are only responsible for the wrongdoing we bring about ourselves, as individual agents, the result would appear to be that no one is responsible for the wrongdoing we collectively cause, thus leaving some of the greatest wrongs without assignable culprits.[12] If we are to avoid this conclusion, we will need to take recourse to theories of *moral complicity*. In the remainder of this section I will briefly discuss two such theories: Kutz's "intentional participation" theory and Lepora and Goodin's "causal contribution" theory. I will remain agnostic as to which of these theories is more convincing regarding the *ground* of complicity, as deciding this matter goes far beyond the scope of this chapter. I believe that both theories allow me to establish that civil servants can be complicit in government wrongdoing and thus to make the central argument that civil servants who are complicit in classified government wrongdoing may have a *pro tanto* obligation to disclose such wrongdoing. In other words, the main argument of the chapter stands, whether one focuses on contribution to harm or on intentional participation. That said, however, I will be working with Lepora and Goodin's account of complicity for the remainder of this chapter. The reason for this is that they view complicity as a function of several factors (mentioned above), allowing us to better establish *degrees* of complicity (and thus to establish obligations to disclose of varying strength).

According to Kutz, the "*intentional participation* in a collective venture is a basis for accountability for the harms and wrongs that result from this venture."[13] He calls this the *complicity principle*. Rather than focusing on the causal contribution an agent has made to the wrongdoing of another, Kutz thus focuses on the content of the agent's will.[14] Participants in collective harms are complicit in and thus accountable for the suffering such harms cause, "not because of the individual differences they make, but because their intentional participation in a collective endeavor directly links them to the consequences of that endeavor."[15]

Yet, critics have pointed out that by viewing a participatory intention as crucial for complicity in joint actions, Kutz risks running together co-principals and complicit agents.[16] Co-principals devise and execute a plan together (i.e., they intend to participate in criminal activity together), whereas a complicit agent "merely" contributes to the wrongdoing of the principal. Say the President and the Secretary of Defense plan an unnecessary and unjust war together. They act as co-principals. Many in the military, as well as civil servants in the executive branch, will be called upon to do their part in implementing this plan of theirs, thus contributing to the co-principals' wrongdoing. When they do so knowingly, meaning that they foresee that their actions will contribute to the wrongdoing in question (the unnecessary and unjust war), they are *complicit* in the principals' wrongdoing. Lepora and Goodin thus provide the following minimum condition for being complicit in another's wrongdoing: "*voluntarily* [i.e., not under duress] performing an action that contributes to the wrongdoing of another and knowing that it does so."[17]

But, Kutz might counter that Lepora and Goodin's causal contribution theory of complicity runs into problems when confronted with cases in which the effects are overdetermined. Consider Parfit's 'Harmless Torturers' example: whereas in the past each of the thousand torturers would inflict severe pain on one of the thousand victims by turning a switch a thousand times, now each torturer turns the switch once for each of the thousand victims: "The victims suffer the same severe pain. But none of the torturers makes any victim's pain perceptibly worse."[18] Each of the torturers can say that his actions did not contribute to the harm inflicted; if one torturer had refused to turn the switch, the pain would not have been perceptibly less. Yet, we still believe the torturers' actions are wrong. It is because of such cases that Kutz proposes to abandon the requirement of causal contribution and to adopt instead the requirement of intentional participation in collective wrongdoing. On his account, the torturers are thus complicit in the wrongdoing, because they intentionally participate in a collective scheme aimed at inflicting severe harm on people.

Lepora and Goodin, instead, resort to the notion of "counterfactual individual difference-making" to assign individual responsibility in such overdetermined cases. Consider the case of the backup assassin:[19] *A* plans to kill *C*. In case he does not succeed, he has hired *B* to kill *C* as a backup. As it happens, *A*'s bullet kills *C*, and so *B* need not fire. Though *B* did not causally contribute to the principal *A*'s wrongdoing, *B* could not have known this in advance. Events might well have unfolded differently (perhaps if *A* was not such a good shot and missed *C*; or perhaps if *A*'s bullet hit *C* but was not a lethal blow), in which case *B* *would* have contributed to the wrongdoing. Given that, as Lepora and Goodin point out, morality ought to be action guiding, its prescriptions must be informed by what the agent could have known *ex ante* rather than in hindsight. At the moment of acting, it was reasonable for *B* to believe that his role would be "potentially essential" to the wrongful outcome. *B* is, therefore, a "counterfactual difference-maker."[20]

In this manner, Lepora and Goodin argue, they can retain their view of complicity as a contribution to wrongdoing, *and* sidestep the pitfall of running together co-principals and complicit agents, as they accuse Kutz of doing. For the remainder of this chapter, I will set aside the question of which of the various theories of moral complicity is the most convincing concerning the *ground* of complicity. Instead, my reason for working with Lepora and Goodin's account in what follows is merely that it allows me to demonstrate how varying degrees of complicity may be established.

Complicity is not all-or-nothing; rather, it comes in degrees, as does the moral blameworthiness for it. Lepora and Goodin propose to view the blameworthiness for an act of complicity as a function of (1) the badness of the principal wrongdoing, (2) the responsibility for the contributory act, (3) the extent of the contribution, and (4) the extent of a shared purpose with the principal wrongdoer.[21] The badness factor is fairly straightforward: how morally wrong is the wrongdoing in question? Is one complicit in the nonviolent theft of a small sum of money or rather in the perpetration of genocide? The responsibility factor is a function of voluntariness – meaning the act was performed freely (i.e., not under duress) and not by accident (i.e., the knowledge that one is contributing to wrongdoing, and the knowledge that the principal wrongdoing is indeed wrong). The contribution factor concerns the extent of the causal contribution made by one's actions to the principal wrongdoing. The shared purpose factor, finally, states that one is more morally blameworthy if one shares in the wrongful purposes of the principal wrongdoer. I will set this last factor aside, however, as I am not convinced sharing a wrongful purpose makes one's complicity worse. Consider the case of Adolf Eichmann: according to Hannah Arendt's account, Eichmann did not contribute to the Holocaust out of rabid anti-Semitism. He was simply an ambitious man who, furthermore, felt that it was his duty as a law-abiding citizen to unquestioningly follow orders.[22] Would we really argue that he was less morally blameworthy because he did not share the Nazis' wrongful purposes? It is not clear to me that someone who knows that there are no good moral reasons for the Holocaust (indeed, there are obviously clear moral prohibitions *against* it!) but contributes to it anyway – out of ambition or a desire for monetary gain, for example[23] – is morally less blameworthy than someone who is obsessed by the idea of the 'Final Solution' and thus shares the Nazis' purposes.[24]

2. *Civil servants are responsible for government wrongdoing, to the extent that they are complicit in it*

Now that we have an idea of what makes one complicit in collective wrongdoing as well as how to measure the extent of one's responsibility for such wrongdoing, we can now turn to the question of *civil servants'* responsibility for *government* wrongdoing, whereby I will focus specifically on unjust laws and policies that are *secret* in nature. The reason for this focus is that no one but those in the know – i.e., politicians and civil servants with the necessary security clearance – could possibly do anything about such wrongdoing. The information being classified, citizens cannot pressure government by protesting or hold it to account by voting it out of office, nor can the press perform its critical function, for the simple reason that both the citizenry and the Fourth Estate are unaware of the wrongdoing in question. The persistence of the unjust laws or policies is, for this reason, attributable to none but the relevant government officials and civil servants. Of these two, I will focus on civil servants as they are typically *complicit* in the wrongdoing of others, namely the government officials who act as principals, rather than acting as (co-)principals themselves.[25]

An additional reason for focusing on *classified* government wrongdoing is that, in Daniel Ellsberg's words, "wrongful secret-keeping is the most widespread form of complicity in wrong-doing. It involves many more people both within and outside an organization that is acting wrongfully than those who give wrongful orders or who directly implement them, though it includes these."[26] This will allow us to speak not only of those who contribute to wrongdoing directly, but also of those who do so by omission, namely through "calculated silence."[27]

To get a better grasp of the wrongdoing I wish to focus on, some examples may be in order. Consider the secret prisons ("black sites") in Eastern Europe during the Bush presidency, where alleged "unlawful enemy combatants" were held and possibly tortured. Members of the civil service and the military must have been involved in this operation concerning matters of logistics, obtaining permission from the "hosting" countries, and drafting the very plans for this operation. Consider as well Justice Department lawyers who advised the CIA, the Department of Defense, and President George W. Bush on the use of enhanced interrogation techniques (such as waterboarding and sleep deprivation) that are generally considered to constitute torture. They also recommended classifying captured prisoners in Iraq and Afghanistan as "enemy combatants" in order to be able to deny them the protections offered by the Geneva conventions. In both these cases, it is likely that the civil servants involved did not initiate the wrongdoing; they were not its principal agents. Instead, they performed the tasks they were ordered to, which contributed to the execution of secret policies that involved wrongdoing. Due to this contribution, they are to be held (partially) responsible for the wrongdoing in question.

Yet, some might say that, while it is fine to hold individuals responsible for their contribution to collective wrongdoing, the specific role of civil servants excludes such an attribution of responsibility. One reason could be that civil servants are expected to be *neutral*: they ought to serve governments of different political persuasions equally well. Their main role obligation is understood to consist in the carrying out of their superiors' commands: "The honor of the civil servant is vested in his ability to execute conscientiously the order of the superior authorities, exactly as if the order agreed with his own conviction."[28] Civil servants are not expected to engage in independent moral reasoning, it is said, but to be malleable instruments of their superiors' will.[29] As such, they cannot be held accountable for their contributions to government wrongdoing.

I have serious doubts that this is an adequate description of civil servants. Not only does this view greatly underestimate the discretion – and thus the independent moral judgment – that civil servants may exercise, but it is also mistaken concerning the object of their loyalty. American civil servants, for example, do not swear to obey their superiors in everything; rather, they solemnly swear to "support and defend the Constitution of the United States against all enemies, foreign and domestic."[30] Furthermore, the first of the basic obligations of the civil service speaks of loyalty to the Constitution, the laws and ethical principles, not of loyalty to one's superiors.[31] Neither the depiction of civil servants as mere instruments of their superiors' wills nor the identification of their central role obligation as consisting in loyalty to superiors is thus correct, allowing us to set this counterargument aside.

A second possible argument against viewing civil servants as complicit and thus partially responsible for government wrongdoing is what Dennis Thompson has called the "excuse from alternative cause":[32] if I hadn't done it, somebody else would have. This is similar to the overdetermined cases discussed above, in that the civil servant who invokes this reasoning argues that her actions were not causally necessary for the wrongdoing to occur, given that someone else would have performed those same actions if she had not. However she acted, in other words, it would have made no difference to the final outcome (even if she had resigned). With Lepora and Goodin we can say, however, that her actions are *potentially essential*. After all, it is not unimaginable, viewed in prospect, that her actions would be causally necessary for the realization of the wrongdoing (perhaps others would have resigned or refused to implement the unjust policy; or perhaps they would have succeeded in convincing their superiors to change the policy), and therefore she remains a "counterfactual individual difference-maker."

A third counterargument states that a civil servant cannot be held accountable for their part in realizing government wrongdoing if they did not know they were contributing to wrongdoing. This argument has some merit. Given the highly compartmentalized structure of modern bureaucracies, it is indeed possible that an individual civil servant did not know that her actions would contribute to government wrongdoing.[33] She was simply doing her job. Here the relevant question, however, is whether she *should* have known. There is such a thing as culpable ignorance. If she stuck her head in the sand, because she did not want to deal with knowing an uncomfortable truth, then she is still morally blameworthy for failing to sufficiently examine the organization she works for and her role in it. In fact, given the great responsibility public servants assume toward the public, we may expect that they go to greater lengths than ordinary citizens in considering the possible consequences of their actions. Given the impact their actions have on general welfare, we are justified in expecting a higher standard.[34] In sum, ignorance can only function as an excuse if it is not negligible.

Having considered and rejected these three possible counterarguments, we may conclude that civil servants can indeed be held responsible for government wrongdoing, to the extent that they are complicit in it.

3. *Responsibility for wrongdoing gives rise to obligations of remedy*

In small-scale, direct interactions between people, the statement that wrongdoing results in obligations of remedy requires little argument: if I am not paying sufficient attention to traffic, causing me to crash into the car in front of me, I incur an obligation to pay for the damage I have caused. If I promise to pick up my daughter at school and forget to do so, I incur an obligation to make amends (by apologizing, or taking her out for ice cream, for example). Though the wrongdoing in question, and particularly one's role in it, is less clear in the case of collective wrongdoing, we have nonetheless established in Section 1 that being complicit in collective wrongdoing results in bearing responsibility for that wrongdoing. Accordingly, contributing to collective wrongdoing also results in the incurrence of obligations of remedy.

4. *The most effective way to remedy classified government wrongdoing is generally by disclosing it*

Now that we have established that civil servants are complicit in government wrongdoing for which they may be held responsible, and as a consequence of which they incur obligations of remedy, we are presented with the rather practical question of how a given civil servant could fulfill this obligation most *effectively*. The actions that allow us to fulfill the obligation of remedy most effectively will generally be understood to be those actions most likely to bring about the end of the wrongful policy.

As a first step, one can of course address the wrongdoing internally and hope one succeeds in convincing those in charge to reform the wrongful policy. If one does succeed, this is a very effective way of fulfilling one's obligation of remedy. The wrongdoing has then ceased. The problem with this approach is that its success depends entirely on one's superiors' susceptibility to critique as well as their willingness to change course. If this course of action does not succeed, however, one could try lodging one's complaint with an external supervisory body. Here, too, however, success may depend on the willingness of the organization to act on the conclusions of the said supervisory body (unless they are legally binding in some way). As a third option, one could request a different assignment, arguing that one does not feel comfortable working on the wrongful policy any longer. Alternatively, one could resign from one's post entirely. Note that these two latter strategies do not so much provide a remedy for the wrongful policy as a means of appeasing the civil servant's own conscience. If requesting a different assignment and resigning does not result in remedying the wrongdoing, one may wonder if the motive of such actions is not so much the desire to remedy wrongdoing as "simply a self-righteous desire to be, or appear, morally 'pure'."[35]

A fifth possible way of fulfilling one's obligation of remedy is by exercising what Arthur Applbaum has called "official discretion."[36] This does not do away with the wrongful policy, but softens its blows or makes the execution of the policy less efficient, thus doing less harm. Civil servants could, for example, withhold information or expertise necessary for executing the policy, and at the same time refuse to step aside so that others may step in to better implement the policy. Note, however, that this strategy does not result in the discontinuation of the policy either. The policy remains in place and the wrongdoing continues, though one does one's best to limit its impact. Most likely, furthermore, one's superiors will be able to discover who is obstructing the policy and find someone more willing to comply.

For a sixth strategy, recall that we are interested in cases of *secret* government wrongdoing, that is, wrongdoing that is brought about through classified policies. Recent history has demonstrated that when the press and subsequently the public at large get wind of their government's wrongful secret policies, they will apply significant pressure on the government to repeal or reform the policy in question, often with success. Thus, the sixth way of fulfilling one's obligation of remedy is by means of informing the public of secret government wrongdoing, that is, by means of unauthorized disclosures. That this strategy can be effective is demonstrated, for example, by the case of Edward Snowden. Following Snowden's revelations, Congress passed the USA Freedom Act, which introduced vital reforms to the NSA's bulk data collection program, the UN General Assembly declared online privacy to be a fundamental human right,[37] and a great public debate concerning the fundamental values of privacy, security, and transparency took place.

In sum, of the six discussed ways of fulfilling one's obligation of remedy, unauthorized disclosures appear to be the most effective. However, we need not make the empirically contestable claim that it is *always* the most effective method. Rather, we can more modestly conclude the following.

5. *Civil servants who are complicit in classified government wrongdoing (and can thus be held responsible for it) incur an obligation to disclose such wrongdoing when disclosure is the most effective way of addressing the wrongdoing*

Or is this conclusion premature? After all, having established that unauthorized disclosures present the most effective way of fulfilling complicit civil servants' obligations of remedy does not yet establish the permissibility of this tactic. For instance, the Allies may have had a duty to beat Nazi Germany and Imperial Japan, and the firebombing of Dresden and the atomic bombing of Hiroshima and Nagasaki may have been the most effective ways of fulfilling that duty (let us suppose), but this does not automatically mean that those bombings were, therefore, also permissible. Regarding unauthorized disclosures, one might argue that one has other obligations to *refrain* from such disclosures, thus barring one from fulfilling one's obligation of remedy in this manner. Let us consider this first counterargument, which we may call the *violation of obligation objection.*

Indeed, as we have seen in Chapter 2, unauthorized disclosures are, in fact, *not* permissible, as they involve a breach of (1) promissory obligations and (2) the obligation to respect the democratic allocation of power.[38] However, we also saw that these obligations are defeasible. Accordingly, they may be defeated by the obligation to provide a remedy for one's contribution to classified government wrongdoing. The civil servant complicit in such wrongdoing incurs an obligation of remedy – which, in general, can be most effectively fulfilled by means of unauthorized disclosures – that can defeat her obligation to respect state secrecy. The latter obligation is thus a *pro tanto* obligation, liable to be defeated by other moral reasons, in this case the obligation to make amends for one's contribution to government wrongdoing by disclosing the said wrongdoing.

Still, this does not mean one can simply proceed to disclose documents. In Chapter 3 we argued that there are three conditions that acts of whistleblowing must meet if they are to be justified. Those conditions apply here as well. First of all, the *public interest condition*: one might have an obligation of remedy and that obligation may be most effectively fulfilled by means of whistleblowing, but if the harm involved in the disclosure of wrongdoing (to the public interest or to particularly weighty private interests) outweighs the benefits to the public interest that disclosure is expected to bring, the best course of action may, all things considered, be to refrain from whistleblowing. If the disclosure would "out" agents in the field, for example, or if the disclosure revealed sensitive military intelligence (that did not point to wrongdoing), and if it is not possible to reveal the wrongdoing without causing such harm (by diligently editing the information and, for example, removing all names of agents and legitimate secrets, as the *minimize harm condition* requires of us), one ought to refrain from whistleblowing and pursue instead one of the alternative ways to fulfill one's obligation of remedy (assuming that the harms mentioned outweigh the benefit to the public interest), even though they may be less effective. Similarly, the *ultimum remedium* condition still applies: before disclosing classified documents to the public, one ought to try addressing the wrongdoing internally first; if that fails, one can take one's complaint to an independent, external oversight body. And only if both of these institutional methods of addressing wrongdoing fail (or are held to be infeasible), may one fulfill one's obligation of remedy by means of unauthorized disclosure. In short, one may have an obligation of remedy that may be most effectively fulfilled by whistleblowing, but one is allowed to use this manner of fulfilling one's obligation only if one has complied with the three justifying conditions of whistleblowing.

Regarding the question of harm, some might say that the average civil servant will not be a particularly good judge of whether a secret policy does indeed involve grave government wrongdoing and of whether disclosure involves impermissible harm to national security or third parties. It is argued that lower-level civil servants in particular may not have access to all the relevant information necessary to make an adequate judgment. This is the *epistemic constraints objection*, discussed and refuted in the previous chapter. In brief, it was pointed out in that chapter that, first, there are many cases of relatively straightforward wrongdoing (e.g. Watergate, the torture at Abu Ghraib, and ordinary political corruption), whereby the fact that the individual civil servant does not possess all the facts is not an obstacle for adequate moral judgment. Second, often a civil servant may resort to whistleblowing *precisely because* the institutional procedures that are normally followed (and that, per Estlund, result in authoritative commands due to their "effort and tendency to get the right answer"[39]) are set aside. In such cases, the counterargument no longer applies, given that the very procedure that is supposed to result in authoritative commands has been bypassed.

Two closely related objections to the conclusion that civil servants who are complicit in classified government wrongdoing incur an obligation to disclose it – the *reasonable disagreement objection* and the *incommensurability of interests objection* – have been elaborately discussed and refuted in the previous chapter as well and so I will not revisit them here. Instead, let us turn to further considerations of harm in order to discuss a final objection. Earlier we argued that harm to others or to the public interest may compel one to refrain from whistleblowing. But, of course, leaking or whistleblowing could also have very harmful consequences for the leaker or whistleblower themselves. Doing the right thing can involve great costs to oneself and one's family. Civil servants who have spoken out have often experienced harsh reprisals, including personal harassment, dismissal, blacklisting, transfer, and criminal charges.[40] Faced with such prospects, a civil servant may understandably opt to remain silent. This brings us to the *overdemandingness objection*. This objection states that it is simply asking too much of people to say that they are obligated to risk their career, their (and thus their family's) income, and possibly even their freedom.

The overdemandingness objection, then, appears to say that unauthorized disclosures are beyond duty, that is, amount to acts of *supererogation*: they are good but not required. Though supererogatory acts are understood to certainly be of moral worth, they are "strictly optional from the standpoint of duty,"[41] and do not, therefore, give rise to culpability when one does not perform them. Obligations of remedy, however, are *not* optional excellences, and their violation *does* result in moral blameworthiness. Disclosing government wrongdoing is thus not a supererogatory act, but rather an obligation. An obligation, however, that is defeasible, as we have seen, and may thus be outweighed by countervailing moral reasons, such as avoiding harm to others and to the public interest. Similarly, harm that may accrue to one's family, for instance, as a consequence of one's disclosures – in a more or less decent state usually not actual physical harm, but certainly professional, financial, legal, and/or psychological harm[42] – should also be taken into account. The same goes for harm to oneself (one's interests, career, and well-being, for example). Thus, if the harmful consequences are sufficiently bad, either for one's loved ones or oneself (or both), they may outweigh the obligation to disclose government wrongdoing in which one is complicit. Recall, however, that complicity is not all-or-nothing but a matter of degree. As a consequence, the obligation resulting from one's complicity in wrongdoing will vary in strength as well, based on the degree of moral blameworthiness for one's complicity. Accordingly, it becomes more difficult for the obligation of remedy to be outweighed by harm considerations the more blameworthy one's complicity is and thus the stronger one's *pro tanto* obligation of remedy is.

Now, one might observe that the several elements being weighed here are not entirely commensurable. After all, how is one to weigh the harm that one might suffer as a consequence of one's disclosure, on the one hand, against the detriment to the public interest caused by the policy in which one is complicit, on the other? Regrettably, this is not an exact science. Still, there are some things we can say. For example, if one is complicit in the waging of an unjust war whereby many civilians lose their lives unbeknownst to the general public, and the harm one will likely suffer upon disclosure is loss of employment, then it seems, intuitively at least, that one's obligation of remedy is not outweighed: loss of employment does not outweigh the loss of innocent lives (though it might still matter how blameworthy one's complicity is, a matter we will further explore in the following section). Conversely, if the personal cost of disclosure is increased (say, an attempt on one's life), and the wrongfulness of the act in which one is complicit is significantly diminished (say, the one-time embezzlement of a small amount of public funds), then the obligation of remedy *is* outweighed. In both these cases, furthermore, the overdemandingness objection misses its mark: in the latter case, overdemandingness is not an issue, because the obligation to disclose is outweighed by the expected harm. In the former case, the obligation stands, yet is not overdemanding. Recall that the obligation to disclose is incurred as a consequence of my contribution to wrongdoing. It is thus not a matter of beneficence, but of justice. I am not innocent, but rather complicit in grave wrongdoing that involves serious harm to others and/or the public interest. Quite a bit may therefore be demanded of me without the obligation becoming overdemanding. Or as Robert Goodin put it: "a morality demanding only what is morally due can hardly be castigated for that."[43]

Finally, if overdemandingness is a concern, we could take steps to make it easier for civil servants to perform their obligations: "Changing the background conditions against which people act – through law, public policy, and the changing behavior of others – is an essential ingredient to lowering the costs for individuals to comply with norms."[44] In the specific case of the obligation to disclose government wrongdoing, government agencies ought to make it possible to voice dissent internally in a meaningful way (i.e., if one's complaint has merit, something is done about it) and without consequences, and states could introduce comprehensive whistleblower protection legislation. In fact, one could argue that the impossibility of voicing dissent internally leads people to pursue alternatives, such as public disclosures. Similarly, the lack of protection for whistleblowers who follow the official procedure leads to people opting for leaks instead, as it is perceived to involve fewer risks. In addition to these organizational and legal changes, some have argued that a change in social ethos is required. This could best be done, it is proposed, by imposing a legal *duty* on civil servants to disclose wrongdoing. In this manner, the law would clearly communicate to all civil servants and, in fact, to the world at large that whistleblowing can be a social good,[45] thus doing away with the still common association of whistleblowers with traitors and snitches.[46]

With these various counterarguments refuted, the conclusion stands that civil servants complicit in government wrongdoing can be under an obligation to disclose that wrongdoing. How to determine the strength of this obligation, and thus the likelihood of its being defeated, is the topic of the next section.

6. *The strength of the* pro tanto *obligation of civil servants who are complicit in classified government wrongdoing to disclose such wrongdoing varies in accordance with (1) the gravity of the wrongdoing in question, (2) one's responsibility for that wrongdoing, and (3) one's contribution to the wrongdoing.*

Having established that the obligation to disclose wrongdoing is defeasible and may thus be "outweighed" by countervailing moral reasons, it becomes all the more important for us to say something more about the strength – or rather the "weight," to stay with the metaphor – of this obligation. If the obligation is very strong, it becomes less likely that it will be outweighed. Conversely, if the obligation is quite weak, it will be that much more likely that it will be defeated by competing moral reasons. In Section 1 we already mentioned that complicity is not binary but instead comes in degrees. Accordingly, the obligation resulting from one's complicity in wrongdoing will vary in strength based on the degree of moral blameworthiness for one's being complicit. The basic idea is: the more blameworthy one's complicity, the stronger one's *pro tanto* obligation of remedy, and the more difficult it will be for this obligation to be outweighed by other (moral) considerations.

Recall that for Lepora and Goodin the blameworthiness for an act of complicity is a function of (1) the badness of the principal wrongdoing, (2) the responsibility for the contributory act, (3) the extent of the contribution, and (4) the extent of a shared purpose with the principal wrongdoer. Recall, too, that I argued to keep the shared purpose factor out of the equation.

Let us then turn to two examples of complicity in government wrongdoing so that we can see how we may assess the strength of the ensuing obligation to disclose that wrongdoing. Consider, first, the case of a lawyer (let's call her Martha) in the U.S. Office of Legal Counsel (OLC), which argued, in the so-called "Torture Memos," that the "enhanced interrogation techniques" (i.e., techniques widely regarded as torture, such as sleep deprivation, stress positions, and waterboarding) the CIA wished to employ in the aftermath of 9/11 were legal, despite their clear contravention of the Geneva Conventions and the United Nations Convention Against Torture and Other Cruel, Inhuman or Degrading Treatment or Punishment.

1. *The badness factor*

I believe it is rather uncontroversial that torture is extremely bad. It is, furthermore, doubtful that information acquired through torture is reliable. But even if it *were* reliable, it is widely agreed that the prohibition on torture is an *absolute* human right, allowing for no exceptions (as opposed to for instance the right to free speech, which may be limited in the case of hate speech, for example). The wrongdoing to which the OLC lawyers contributed – i.e., numerous violations of an absolute human right – is thus extremely morally wrong.

2. *The responsibility factor*

Recall that the responsibility factor is a function of voluntariness, the knowledge that one is contributing to wrongdoing, and the knowledge that the principal wrongdoing is indeed wrong. Regarding the voluntariness, one imagines that the OLC as a whole experienced pressure from both the CIA and the Bush administration to contort the law in such a way as to make torture legally possible. As a consequence, individual lawyers within the OLC may have felt under pressure not to provide dissenting legal views. Still, such pressure cannot qualify as duress. After all, the very function of the OLC is to provide *independent* legal advice to the President and the executive branch agencies. The possibility that the executive or one's direct superior in the OLC is not pleased with the advice provided may be awkward or even result in extreme unpleasantness, but that does still not amount to a situation of duress. Our OLC lawyer thus acted voluntarily.

Did Martha know she was *contributing* to wrongdoing? When the CIA repeatedly comes to the Office you work for requesting reassurances – following official Bush administration statements that the US does not mistreat its prisoners, for example – that what it's doing is legal,[47] you can be sure that your legal advice is an important contribution to the CIA's actions.

Finally, Martha knew that the CIA was employing interrogation techniques that are ordinarily categorized as torture, and, as said, the idea that torture is wrong is rather straightforward. That Martha knew this becomes apparent from the fact that she and her colleagues bent over backwards in order to be able to say that the CIA's interrogation techniques did *not* constitute torture. Still, it is possible that she knew all this, but viewed torture as a necessary evil in order to keep the country safe. Accordingly, she may have viewed the torture to be justified. This is a possible position. In the best-case scenario, therefore, she believed the torture to be a justified wrong; in the worst-case scenario, she believed the torture to be simply wrong, but provided legal advice that enabled it anyway, because of prudential reasons (concerns about her career, peer pressure, not wanting to be the only dissenting voice, and so forth).

3.   *The contribution factor*[48]

The centrality of one's contribution is determined by (1) the magnitude of one's contribution to the principal wrongdoing and (2) the probability that one's contribution will be essential for the wrongdoing to succeed.[49] Regarding, first, the magnitude of the contribution, the OLC as a whole provided the legal cover for the CIA's torture program. This contribution, second, was certainly essential. The fact that the CIA kept requesting reassurances from the OLC that what it was doing was legal demonstrates that it was very uneasy about its activities. Therefore, "had *anyone* had the temerity to say no, the program almost certainly would have halted."[50] Furthermore, judgments concerning the legality of the torture program were uniquely in the executive's hands, as the other branches of government and the public at large were unaware of its existence. As a result, "on the question of torture the OLC lawyers were the last – and only – line of defense, since the detainees were denied all recourse to the outside world."[51]

Let us assume that our *individual* lawyer within the OLC, Martha, had been ordered to go through the relevant national and international case law concerning torture and cruel, inhuman, degrading treatment to see if she could find any way to conclude that the CIA's interrogation methods were legal. Certainly, the OLC's final advice consisted of more than her contribution alone; other lawyers were working on the matter as well. Furthermore, had she refused to perform this task, others at the OLC would have taken her place. Her refusal would thus not have been likely to change the final outcome. Still, as it was, Martha *did* contribute to the OLC's final advice, which was absolutely essential to the success of the wrongdoing in question. As such, she was complicit in and incurred responsibility for the wrongdoing. Her complicity, and thus her responsibility, may vary, however, according to the importance of her contribution. It is hard to quantify this exactly, but we can at least say that she is less complicit and thus less responsible if we assume that she worked on this legal advice with ten other lawyers than if she had worked on it by herself, as (1) the magnitude of her contribution would be smaller in the former case. Similarly, we can say that (2) her contribution would be more essential to the wrongdoing if she had drafted the advice on her own than if she had done so with ten of her colleagues. Here, I will assume that she worked together with her colleagues, rather than by herself.

To recap: (1) the wrongdoing in question was highly wrong; (2) the contribution to the wrongdoing was voluntary, Martha knew she was contributing to the CIA's torture program, and she knew that torture is wrong, though she may have viewed it as a necessary evil; (3) she contributed to the OLC's legal advice that was, in Lepora and Goodin's terms, "definitely causally essential" to the wrongdoing (that is, "a necessary condition for the wrong to take place"[52]), but she was not the sole contributor to that advice, plus she could have been replaced by someone else if she had refused to contribute.

Given the severity of the wrong, and the fact that Martha freely and knowingly contributed to it, her complicity is very blameworthy, though it is mitigated by the fact that she did not act alone. Still, her contribution to grave wrongdoing results in an obligation of remedy that is quite strong. Accordingly, her obligation to disclose the wrongdoing will not easily be outweighed by the possible harm that will accrue to her and her family if she discloses the information to the public. We are talking about complicity in the legalization of torture, that is, severe physical harm that "shocks the conscience." It is doubtful that the loss of one's job, for example, or even possible disbarment, weigh up against the enabling of such grossly unjust acts. Of course, before disclosing the information, one ought to first exhaust the alternatives to public disclosure (as per the *ultimum remedium* condition). Furthermore, one ought to still take care to remove all information not strictly required to reveal the wrongdoing (as per the minimize harm condition).

Let us then turn to a second example: our OLC lawyer Martha is now a relatively low-level employee (if such distinctions exist within the OLC), who is merely asked to provide a review of the relevant case law concerning conflicts of interest in government. Subsequently, her review is used to provide legal cover for a relatively minor conflict of interest of the President. Now, concerning the *badness factor*: though conflicts of interests are of course to be strictly avoided, the wrongdoing in question is certainly less unjust than the CIA torture program, particularly since it is a minor conflict of interest and, let us further assume, the only one. Regarding the *responsibility factor*: though Martha does know that conflicts of interests are wrong, she does not know she is being asked to contribute to providing the President with legal cover for her conflict of interest, which is being diligently kept out of the public eye. Perhaps Martha ought to have known, but let us assume that, though it was possible to find out the true reason behind the request made to her, this would have been quite difficult. Her *contribution*, lastly, is very important, as she found an exemption for the president from conflict-of-interest laws. Without this legal cover, the president would remove the conflicting property. Other people working at the OLC, however, could have found that exemption equally well and would have if Martha had not.

In this case, the blameworthiness of Martha's complicity is far less great. As a consequence, the obligation to disclose this wrongdoing (let us assume she later finds out about the conflict of interest and her role in allowing it to occur) to the public is less strong and can be outweighed more easily by considerations of the possible financial, professional, and psychological harm to herself and her family.

These two examples have thus shown how the *pro tanto* obligation of remedy can vary in strength as one's complicity is judged to be more or less blameworthy, which will make it more or less difficult, respectively, for this *pro tanto* obligation to be defeated.

The (not so) separate question of bystanders

Thus far we have considered the responsibility of civil servants who are complicit in government wrongdoing by actively contributing to it. But what about those who do not actively contribute, but who are aware of the wrongdoing in question? Imagine our OLC lawyer, Martha, does not contribute to the "Torture Memos," but is aware of what her colleagues are working on, and thus, let us assume, of the CIA torture program. This is analogous to the proverbial child drowning in the pond: Martha is a bystander to wrongdoing and has the means to at least attempt to do something about it. She could disclose the wrongdoing, which could well (but need not) result in a public outcry, investigative Congressional hearings, and, eventually, the repeal of the torture program. The questions are: does she have an obligation to blow the whistle or to leak the information to the press? Is her silence blameworthy? We have said earlier, in following Lepora and Goodin's account of moral complicity, that the obligation of remedy arises from one's contribution to wrongdoing: if I did not slam into your car and had nothing at all to do with the accident, I am under no obligation to pay to have it fixed. As a bystander, Martha did not contribute to the wrongdoing: she wasn't involved in drafting the plans to expand the permitted interrogation techniques, she did not herself carry out torture, and she did not draft the OLC memo providing legal cover. It would thus seem she incurs no obligation to reveal the wrongdoing.

Yet, omissions can also be causally effective: my omitting to save the child in the pond when I easily could have, certainly contributes to her death. Similarly, Martha's silence made it possible for the wrongdoing to continue. In that sense, she contributed to and is complicit in torture. For this reason, I argue, Martha *does* have an obligation to disclose the secret torture program, even as a bystander. Intuitively, however, it seems we should say that her obligation to do so is weaker than those of her colleagues who actually contributed to the provision of legal cover: after all, if two people (*A* and *B*) are equally in a position to help the drowning child, but *A* (accidentally) pushed the child in, whereas *B* simply happened to be standing there, it would seem that *A* has the stronger obligation of the two to rescue the child. Both may have what we could call a natural duty of assistance, but only one of the two additionally incurs an obligation to help due to her contribution to wrongdoing. Furthermore, one's complicity is greater the more central one's silence is to the continuation of the wrongdoing. If it is certain that the wrongdoing would continue even if you were to disclose it, then one's obligation is weaker than if it is certain that the wrongdoing would cease once (or shortly after) you disclosed it. After all, in the first case it seems one's silence is not an essential contribution for the wrongdoing to succeed, whereas in the latter case it is.[53]

Conclusion

Instead of the more common question whether unauthorized disclosures can ever be permissible, this chapter set out to answer the question whether they can ever be *obligatory*. Specifically, it inquired whether civil servants who are complicit in secret government wrongdoing incur an obligation to disclose the said wrongdoing. This question was answered affirmatively (though the obligation to disclose is still subject to the three justifying conditions of whistleblowing). It was argued that civil servants who are complicit in secret government wrongdoing are under a *pro tanto* obligation to reveal that wrongdoing (when disclosure is the most effective way of addressing it and when the three justifying conditions have been met), the strength of which (and thus the likelihood of its being defeated by countervailing moral reasons) will vary in accordance with (1) the gravity of the wrongdoing, (2) one's responsibility for that wrongdoing, and (3) one's contribution to the wrongdoing. This obligation is, furthermore, not limited to those who actively contribute to wrongdoing, but extends to those who are mere bystanders, whose silence can amount to complicity when it is a causal factor in allowing the wrongdoing to continue.

This may seem to be asking quite a lot of civil servants, given the personal risks involved with whistleblowing and leaking. However, I argued that (1) responsibility for wrongdoing gives rise to obligations of remedy, which may be quite demanding, and (2) that the obligations involved are defeasible, allowing for the possibility of their being outweighed when serious personal harm would result as a consequence of one's unauthorized disclosure. A further argument against the overdemandingness objection would result from a consideration of civil servants' role obligations. Public office is a public trust, which requires "employees to place loyalty to the Constitution, the laws and ethical principles above private gain."[54] Thus, though we can all be said to have, at least on a Rawlsian account, a natural *duty* of justice to support and comply with just institutions that apply to us, civil servants, upon the assumption of their position, additionally incur an *obligation* to support and comply with just institutions, tying them even more tightly to those institutions.[55] We can, in other words, expect more from civil servants when it comes to upholding just institutions, which makes their complicity in wrongdoing that harms those institutions all the more blameworthy. As it is more blameworthy, it becomes less problematic that the ensuing obligation of remedy may be quite demanding.

Notes

1 This chapter draws from Boot, Eric R. 2019. Obligatory Whistleblowing: Civil Servants and the Complicity-Based Obligation to Disclose Government Wrongdoing. *Journal of Moral Philosophy*. 16: 131–159.
2 Kant, Immanuel. 1996. Religion Within the Boundaries of Mere Reason. In *Religion and Rational Theology*. Eds. Allen Wood and Paul Guyer, Trans. George Di Giovanni, 39–215. Cambridge: Cambridge University Press. Ak 6: 49.
3 See Rawls, J. 1999. Legal Obligation and the Duty of Fair Play. In *Collected Papers*. Ed. S. Freeman, 117–29. Cambridge (Mass.): Harvard University Press. 118; also see Hart, H.L.A. 1955. Are There Any Natural Rights? *The Philosophical Review* 64 (2), 175–91. 179n.
4 For example: Delmas, Candice. 2016. Political Resistance for Hedgehogs. In *The Legacy of Ronald Dworkin*. Eds. Wil Waluchow and Stefan Sciaraffa, 25–48. Oxford: Oxford University Press; Parekh, Bhikhu. 1993. A Misconceived Discourse on Political Obligation. *Political Studies* 41: 236–51.
5 See, for example: Delmas, Candice. 2015. The Ethics of Government Whistleblowing. *Social Theory and Practice* 41: 77–105; Sagar, Rahul. 2013. *Secrets and Leaks: The Dilemma of State Secrecy*. Princeton: Princeton University Press; Scheuerman, William E. 2014. Whistleblowing as Civil Disobedience: The Case of Edward Snowden. *Philosophy and Social Criticism* 40: 609–28.
6 Delmas, Candice. 2014. The Civic Duty to Report Crime and Corruption. *Les ateliers de l'éthique* 9: 50–64.
7 Ceva, Emanuela, and Michele Bocchiola. 2018. Personal Trust, Public Accountability, and the Justification of Whistleblowing. *Journal of Political Philosophy*. Advance online publication. doi: 10.1111/jopp.12170.
8 5 C.F.R. § 2635.101(b)(11). In the Netherlands there is a similar law obliging civil servants to report abuses of power and corruption that they encounter in their workplace: Article 162(1) Wetboek van Strafvordering.
9 Davis, Michael. 1996. Some Paradoxes of Whistleblowing. *Business & Professional Ethics Journal* 15: 3–19.
10 Scheffler, S. 2001. Individual Responsibility in a Global Age. In *Boundaries and Allegiances: Problems of Justice and Responsibility in Liberal Thought*, 32–47. Oxford: Oxford University Press. 39. Cf. Singer, P. 1972. Famine, Affluence, and Morality. *Philosophy and Public Affairs*, 1 (3), 229–43. 232; Lichtenberg, J. 2010. Negative Duties, Positive Duties, and the "New Harms." *Ethics*, 120(3), 557–78.

11 Lichtenberg. *New Harms*. 561.
12 Kutz, C. 2000. *Complicity: Ethics and Law for a Collective Age*. Cambridge: Cambridge University Press. 113.
13 Kutz. *Complicity*. 164–5. Emphasis added.
14 Ibid. 165.
15 Ibid. 138.
16 Lepora, C., and R.E. Goodin. 2015. *On Complicity and Compromise*. New York: Oxford University Press. 80.
17 Ibid. 82.
18 Parfit, D. 1984. *Reasons and Persons*. Oxford: Oxford University Press. 80.
19 Lepora and Goodin. *Complicity*. 56–8.
20 Ibid. 65.
21 Ibid. 98.
22 Arendt, H. 1963. *Eichmann in Jerusalem: A Report on the Banality of Evil*. London: Faber & Faber. Ch. 8.
23 Indeed, on a Kantian account, evil does not so much consist in willing evil, but in making "the incentives of self-love and their inclinations the condition of compliance with the moral law" (Kant. *Religion*. Ak 6: 36). This seems an appropriate description of civil servants who contribute to the drafting and execution of unjust laws and policies: the problem is not so much that they all wish to do wrong; rather, they make the satisfaction of their inclinations (to have a successful career, to have high social standing, to have a nice salary) the condition of compliance with morality's commands.
24 Indeed, it seems to me that Lepora and Goodin's own account renders the shared purpose factor irrelevant as well, since they view shared purposes as characteristic of co-principals rather than of complicit agents (a distinction they criticize Kutz for eliding). See, e.g., Lepora and Goodin. *Complicity*. 81.
25 I do not mean to suggest that civil servants can never act as (co-)principals. Rather, I aim to establish the harder case, namely that complicit agents can be held responsible for government wrongdoing. It then goes without saying that, *a fortiori*, civil servants acting as (co-)principals can also be held responsible for wrongdoing.
26 Ellsberg, Daniel. 2013. Secrecy and National Security Whistleblowing. *OpEdNews*, January 17. Retrieved from: http://www.ellsberg.net/archive/secrecy-national-security-whistleblowing.
27 Hill, Thomas E., Jr. 1991. Symbolic Protest and Calculated Silence. In *Autonomy and Self-Respect*, 52–66. Cambridge: Cambridge University Press.
28 Weber, Max. 1991. Politics as a Vocation. In *Essays in Sociology*. Eds. H.H. Gerth and C. Wright Mills, Trans. H.H. Gerth and C. Wright Mills, 77–128. London: Routledge. 95.
29 Quinlan offers a defense of such a view, based on his own experience in the British Civil Service: Quinlan, Michael. 1993. Ethics in the Public Service. *Governance* 6: 538–44.
30 5 US Code § 3331 – Oath of Office.
31 5 C.F.R. § 2635.101(b) – Basic obligation of public service.
32 Thompson, Dennis F. 1980. Moral Responsibility of Public Officials: The Problem of Many Hands. *The American Political Science Review* 74: 905–16. 909.

33 Bovens, M. 1998. *The Quest for Responsibility: Accountability and Citizenship in Complex Organisations*. Cambridge: Cambridge University Press. 126ff. Bovens maintains that the "psychological distance" between a functionary performing their daily tasks and the effects of that performance results in a passivity of conscience.

34 Thompson, Dennis F. 1985. The Possibility of Administrative Ethics. *Public Administration Review* 45: 555–61. 560.

35 Hill. *Symbolic Protest*. 52. Cf. Williams's discussion of "moral self-indulgence": Williams, B. 1981. Utilitarianism and Moral Self-Indulgence. In *Moral Luck*, 40–53. Cambridge: Cambridge University Press.

36 Applbaum, A.I. 1992. Democratic Legitimacy and Official Discretion. *Philosophy & Public Affairs*, 21 (3), 240–74.

37 United Nations General Assembly. *The Right to Privacy in the Digital Age*. U.N. Doc A/RES/68/167 (December 18, 2013).

38 I omit role obligations here, as we saw in Chapter 2 that role obligations, at least on the civic account of civil servants' role obligations, which I endorse, do not militate against unauthorized disclosures if the information disclosed reveals grave government wrongdoing of public interest.

39 Estlund, David. 2007. On Following Orders in an Unjust War. *The Journal of Political Philosophy* 15: 213–34. 221.

40 Glazer, M., and P. Glazer. 1989. *The Whistleblowers: Exposing Corruption in Government and Industry*. New York: Basic Books. For examples of such consequences see especially Chapter 5.

41 Baron, M. 1995. *Kantian Ethics Almost Without Apology*. Ithaca: Cornell University Press. 28n.

42 For a poignant example of the strain wrought on one's family life when one's superiors decide to retaliate as a consequence of one's revelations, see Glazer and Glazer. *The Whistleblowers*. 153ff.

43 Goodin, Robert E. 2009. Demandingness as a Virtue. *The Journal of Ethics* 13: 1–13. 2.

44 Lichtenberg. *New Harms*. 577.

45 Moberly, R. 2012. Whistleblowers and the Obama Presidency: The National Security Dilemma. *Employee Rights and Employment Policy Journal* 16 (51): 51–141. 133.

46 Regarding this common association, see: Worth, M. 2013. *Whistleblowing in Europe: Legal Protections for Whistleblowers in the EU*. Transparency International. 15–18.

47 Cole, David. 2015. Torture: No One Said No. *The New York Review of Books*, March 5. Retrieved from: http://www.nybooks.com/daily/2015/03/05/cia-torture-no-one-said-no/.

48 Here I will not, for reasons of space, discuss all six factors identified by Lepora and Goodin that determine the importance of one's contribution (see, e.g., *Complicity*. 106ff.), but will limit myself to the matter of "centrality."

49 Lepora and Goodin. *Complicity*. 66.

50 Cole. *Torture*.

51 Cole, David. 2009. The Torture Memos: The Case Against the Lawyers. *The New York Review of Books*, October 8. Retrieved from: http://www.nybooks.com/articles/2009/10/08/the-torture-memos-the-case-against-the-lawyers/.

52 Lepora and Goodin. *Complicity*. 66.

53 Notice that a different understanding of the ground of complicity will not necessarily make the bystander case any easier. For example, unsatisfied with the
solution provided above, we might turn to Kutz's account of moral complicity,
which holds that the intentional participation in collective wrongdoing is all
that is required to establish complicity. The fact that Martha, in the bystander
example, does not causally contribute to the wrongdoing (except by viewing
omissions as causally effective as well) is not relevant for Kutz, as "causation is
not necessary to complicity" (Kutz, Christopher. 2007. Causeless Complicity.
Criminal Law and Philosophy 1: 289–305. 290). It may seem that this makes it
easier to view Martha as complicit, as all that is required is that she intentionally participates. But can we view her silence as "participation"? Kutz holds
that intentional participation in collective wrongdoing requires doing one's
part intentionally and viewing one's participation as part of a collective project
(Kutz. *Complicity*. 138). The latter in particular is problematic, as it seems a
stretch to say that the bystander always views their inaction as part of a collective project. On this, also see Driver, Julia. 2015. Kantian Complicity. In
*Reason, Value, and Respect: Kantian Themes from the Philosophy of Thomas
E. Hill, Jr.* Eds. Mark Timmons and Robert N. Johnson, 256–66. Oxford:
Oxford University Press. 260.

54 5 C.F.R. § 2635.101(b) – Basic obligation of public service.

55 Rawls, J. 1999. *A Theory of Justice*. Revised ed. Cambridge (Mass.): Belknap
Press of Harvard University Press. 99–100; cf. 330. Recall the distinction
between duties and obligations, expounded in the very first paragraph of this
chapter.

Index